D0042788

Ctrl Alt Delete

Although this Book is based on numerous real people and real events, some names, places and identifying features have been changed in order to preserve their privacy.

Ctrl Alt Delete
How I Grew Up Online

Emma Gannon

EBURY
PRESS

1 3 5 7 9 10 8 6 4 2

Ebury Press, an imprint of Ebury Publishing
20 Vauxhall Bridge Road
London SW1V 2SA

Ebury Press is part of the Penguin Random House group of companies
whose addresses can be found at global.penguinrandomhouse.com

Penguin
Random House
UK

Copyright © Emma Gannon 2016

Emma Gannon has asserted her right to be identified as the author of this
Work in accordance with the Copyright, Designs and Patents Act 1988

First published by Ebury Press in 2016

www.penguin.co.uk

A CIP catalogue record for this book is available from the British Library

ISBN 9781785032721

Typeset in India by Thomson Digital Pvt Ltd, Noida, Delhi
Printed and bound in Great Britain by Clays Ltd, St Ives PLC

MIX
Paper from
responsible sources
FSC
www.fsc.org   FSC® C018179

Penguin Random House is committed to a sustainable future
for our business, our readers and our planet. This book is
made from Forest Stewardship Council® certified paper.

For teenagers: past and present

contents

Introduction: 'Pics or it didn't happen!'   1

1. Photoshopping Myself   5

2. I Discover Cybersex   26

3. The Day My Friend Got an Internet Boyfriend   46

4. Google Ruins My First IRL Relationship   63

5. Down the Rabbit Hole   80

6. Online Dating Isn't the Same as Online Shopping   103

7. Nice Porn, for Nice People   126

8. Getting an Internet Job   143

9. Just Another WordPress Blog   163

10. If Tinder Was For Friendships   189

11. They Don't Just Exist in Fairy Tales   204

12. Anonymous Was a Woman   221

13. Death in the Digital Age   245

Acknowledgements   259

introduction

'Pics or
it didn't happen!'

That was what someone said to me when I told them I was off to read from my teenage diary in front of a load of people in a pub basement. Hidden behind the humour was a request for proof. I've started to notice that this happens all the time. We obsessively document our lives on social media because the experience itself is now not enough. We basically live face down in pixels and post whatever is in our heads, whenever we want, without a second thought. We're in a constant state of Keeping Up, whether that be with the Kardashians or our own friends, always rushing for the next big thing. Without realising it, we're weighing up our best angles, wittiest captions and finest filters before sharing. Frankly, we are the producers, stylists, camera crew and directors of our own lives. Our own Truman Shows.

There are even people in the world who say the word 'hashtag' out loud.

1

It's scary out there.

It's amazing to think that only eleven years ago, when I was fifteen, it was all about experimenting with emails, illegally downloading Backstreet Boys songs via Napster or LimeWire and playing Snake on a Pay As You Go brick phone that could only churn out 120-character text messages (a good skill to have honed years later when Twitter was invented). I had to fight my parents and sister to use the family computer, located in the family computer room on a desk piled high with blank discs, *Encarta*, *Barbie Fashion Designer* and *Petz* CD-ROMs, the pixelated computer games only requiring the space bar to 'jump' and arrows to move! I had to connect to the Internet via a dial up that would get disconnected every time someone wanted to use the phone!

During these first few years online, I learned to social network way before it was a thing – and it all happened under cover. I was introduced to Bebo, MSN and Myspace, and consequently the embarrassing profiles, incriminating comments and chats (with their dubious statuses: mine was usually *~*EMMA*~*. Witty. Insightful). During those digital discovery years, I was also experimenting with the fact that my online self could appear to be a more glamorous, confident version of me, quite far removed from the realities of who I really was. I learned pretty early on that I could tweak the way my body looked, and, aged thirteen, my best friend and I discovered a free photo-editing tool and we got scarily skilled at it. We'd post the photos online, getting compliments by the dozen.

To be honest, no one really knew what they were doing back then, or where it would eventually lead, and most of it remained a secret. But, looking back now, I'm glad that my teenage self didn't have a smartphone, otherwise I would have definitely posted seventeen selfies a day, all with brown lipstick and horrifi-cally bad hairstyles held up by butterfly clips. One of the mean girls at school would definitely have taken a photo of my 'head-gear' (a massive piece of kit that hooked to my train-track braces in the corners of my mouth and wrapped all the way around my head) and posted it to Instagram with accompanying hashtags #braces #emma #gross. Growing up *with* the Internet was difficult enough anyway, let alone growing up *on* the World Wide Web as young people do today. I'm so glad I don't have those pressures.

At some point during my twenties, I sat on my bed refreshing my Facebook page – hoping for a few more 'likes' – and realised that I wanted to stop living in a shallow world of getting 'hits'. I thought about how we're constantly hungry for the new and now. How we write blog posts, quick quips, tweets and statuses, and how we share links, photos and video, all to help cultivate our own brand. And, most days, I feel overwhelmed by it all. I thought back to my life growing up with the Internet and how it shaped me, and continues to shape me. It was during this 'moment' that I realised that I needed to write something longer than a blog post to acknowledge the long road it has taken me to accept myself, to laugh at my online failures and celebrate the good. No glossiness, no filters, no illusions. I wanted to share my story – the story of an imperfect girl making mistakes in the digital world – to encour-age others to share theirs, and maybe take their own digital world less seriously. I've cringed as I've typed most of this book – but I felt it was important to put it out into the world – and so here is my attempt at proving our generation can write something longer than a tweet. It would be easy to live behind filters, but what would be the fun in that …

'Stop editing your pics. What if you go missing? How can we find you if you look like Beyoncé on Facebook, and Chewbacca in person ...'

@itsWillyFerrell2

chapter 1
Photoshopping Myself

2002

Go on, edit the size of your thighs.
> *It's only a quick retouch.*
> *See, easy.*
> *Actually, while you're at it, edit out that crease on your elbow.*
> *And that eye wrinkle.*
> *And your chin area.*
> *You want to be liked, don't you?*

I am thirteen years old, sitting in front of the family computer, looking at a raw image of myself on the computer and wincing. On the pixelated screen, I run my fingers over the close-up of my face. Surely just a few more touch-ups wouldn't hurt?

As a teenager, I was the clichéd girl standing in front of the full-length mirror in my bedroom, grabbing my puppy fat with my hands and contorting myself to check out every detail of my body with a hand-held mirror. I'd pull my thighs back to imagine a thigh gap, or push my boobs up so I could pretend they sat higher on my body. I'd claw at my chin to try to recreate how models look with their chiselled features. I'd tear out photos of underwear models from magazines and Pritt-Stick them into my dog-eared WHSmith diary. Your standard awkward teen stuff, I suppose.

But I was also dealing with the trials and tribulations of being a sibling to a very slim and perfectly toned sister. I was jealous of Jo because she'd had more lucky numbers in the genetic lottery than me; she was a girl with such a naturally beautiful, toned, flat tummy and long limbs that she would look good at *any angle*. Unlike me, she would not have a droplet of sweat form on the back of her neck when she heard the click of a camera, before feeling obliged to lurch into a flattering 'trick' position to hide the lumps and bumps. Every day I would listen to the constant stream of compliments directed at her, while I shuffled awkwardly, hoping for some of her leftovers. It was hard to slag off Barbie's body as being unrealistic and disproportionate when a very similar Real-Life Version existed next to me, who I loved more than anything.

Of course, my family would probably say that I'm exaggerating, and they would remind me that *you're beautiful in your own way too!* – because that's what people say when they love you. But back then I couldn't fight the feeling of knowing that my 'looks' would never be my defining feature. I would have to fill the deficit by being funny, or loud, or a bit odd, instead. I wasn't mad with Jo about it; it wasn't her fault she was born so perfect, so it would have been unfair for me to take it out on her. But it stung nonetheless.

Where did this anxiety come from? Certainly, some of it came from never receiving the same compliments as my sister or being looked at in the same way. But it also came from the magazines I'd read; the conversations I'd overheard from the boys I knew; the slimming adverts on TV; the way girls at school spoke about food; the lack of comments I received on photos I'd shared online; the comparisons with the looks of the pop singers and film stars I saw on screen. I could go on.

It was my lumps, bumps and veiny bits that had always been my curse, being an extremely pale girl with a penchant for refrigerated KitKats. With glittery moisturiser, an element of self-confidence and an entourage, I knew my big thighs *could* look sexy. But I didn't feel like Beyoncé, I just felt like a heavy seal.

I also had stretch marks scattered all over my boobs from them growing too quickly. They literally grew overnight. I went to bed with a hot chocolate, a book and a concave chest and woke up the next day with a sharp throbbing pain and two new mounds of tissue digging hard into the wiry mattress beneath me. My boobs had erupted as suddenly as a cartoon beanstalk – and with a vengeance. Ironically, just days before it happened, I was lightly bullied in the girls' changing rooms for having 'Tic Tacs' for boobs. (I can no longer look at those iconic little mints in the same way.) Imagine my delight-slash-terror at having to go into school a few days later with a huge pair of boobs knocking around, cupped in a lovely new M&S bra that my mum had bought me, with people poking at my chest convinced I'd stuffed rolled-up tights in there. Before long, the entire class was feeling up my chest, prodding me and exclaiming, 'Oh my God, they're actually real!' and then running off, sniggering. I didn't know what to do with them.

This body anxiety forced me to come up with solutions. I quickly learned that if I positioned myself slightly downhill, with the photographer snapping the shot from above, my legs would look thinner. I would use Sellotape to pin back the flabby bits underneath my arms just to test out how they might look if I was skinny. I would tense my thighs so they were momentarily not touching each other by leaning against a wall and pushing the tops of my hips backwards. I'd push my shoulders back so my boobs pointed upwards.

I longed to be the sort of person who didn't care what they looked like in a photo, but I just couldn't allow myself to be captured on camera without hiding the bits I hated first. My sister and I would have annual photoshoots when we were abroad on our summer holiday, an opportunity for me to go back home armed with at least *some* nice photographs to post on Bebo, the first social network I discovered in 2001. The only aim in mind at this point in my teenage life was to boost my cripplingly low self-esteem and get a few nice comments from the locals via the Internet – you know, maybe even *a boy*. Jo would be enthusiastic at first, snapping away and saying: 'Ooh, I think we got a good one!' She was genuinely pleased to be helping me. But then after a while she'd slump and ask if she could stop because her arms were getting tired and she was getting bored of my constant requests for readjustments and retakes. I sort of felt sorry for her: she suffered from the guilt-factor of always looking good in photos and as a result she felt obliged to commit to getting at least one decent picture of me to shut me up.

It would be extremely unfair to assume Jo had *no* body hang-ups, but I know she was confused by my obsession to get good angles. Maybe she couldn't work out if I was a self-obsessed narcissist or an innocent paranoid android. Maybe a bit of both. But what was clear was that I was insecure and young enough to really buy into the idea that a woman had to Look A Certain Way. I wasn't naturally slim, I had braces and boobs that weren't under my chin – shout out to those women's magazines who promote the idea that your breasts should be able to ignore the laws of gravity – so I was always striving for something else. Something better, something *glossier*.

This was before the days when social media had properly erupted into the thing it is now. No apps, only desktop websites to communicate. On Bebo I had a handful of online 'friends', aka people from down the road who went on their family computer approximately once a month. I noticed early on I was more into the whole *Internet thing* than most other children my age. They really were a 'take it or leave it' bunch. Any risk of judgement about my aesthetics was therefore relatively small. But knowing that photos were starting to be slapped up online for the first time made me feel like I should keep learning new tricks to mask my true body shape.

I can clearly remember the rush I felt when I first edited a photo of myself. I was twelve years old. It was a sunny afternoon in the house in which I grew up in Exeter, and I hunched over the bulky family computer and taught myself for the very first time how to 'rub out' a spot on my face, just like erasing a pencil mark on a piece of paper. It was so easy. I'd been learning how to use Microsoft Paint, how to chisel away at images, cutting pictures out, filling in imperfect gaps. It was incredibly retro but it worked.

Half of the euphoria I felt was due to the fact I had succeeded at stealthily and secretly figuring out *how* to physically do it with the limited tools available, and the other half was elation at just how *good* I looked in the photo as a result.

Oh, we may laugh now, but at the time that little pipette, allowing you to extract the very same colour a millimetre either side of a patchy bit of skin, was my new favourite toy. It was an exciting thing to have discovered during the height of my insecurity.

From that point on, I would erase most of my imperfections, leaving *some* natural marks in, so it didn't look too obvious (I wasn't a fool). I believed no one would ever be the wiser. That was the very early beginnings of my soon-to-be addiction with editing my own photos.

I didn't see any harm in it. It was just a bit of fun, just to make my close-up profile photos look slightly more flattering. In fact it wasn't a big deal at all; this was simply my version of messing around using Clipart in IT lessons. However, there is something terribly screwed up when your 'inspiration' as a twelve-year-old is an unachievable, streamlined version of yourself that you, yourself, edited and printed out. A version of yourself that you could never actually be.

This was the beginning of me feeling I had an online body that I loved and an IRL version that I loathed.

A few years later, I discovered Google's Picasa programme, a photo-editing tool that has since evolved into a photo-sharing network but was originally *meant* to be used for editing wildlife photography or pictures of sunsets. There was a free 'digital tour' of how to use the tool and it made a big song and dance about how it was aimed at photography professionals who perhaps wanted to innocently 'enhance' an already striking photo. It was meant to be for the birdwatchers with the bum bags. Or the posh dads on safari trips with their expensive long lenses and slightly too big khaki shorts, getting close-ups of a moody lion. Essentially it was the 2004 version of an Afterlight or VSCO Cam, with beautiful filter options and an ability to crop perfectly, lighten, sharpen, add saturation, 'warmify' or add a blurry effect that was called 'glow'. The glow option fast became my favourite feature on the whole of Picasa; it would make me and my best friend look as radiant as Audrey Hepburn in a romantic movie close-up. Or perhaps we resembled the sun from the *Teletubbies*, who knows. It was our secret Instagram before Instagram blew up in our faces. On the screen, we loved ourselves.

Only my closest friends knew my dirty little secret. My friend Gwen would come round and ask me to edit her photos, too, as soon as I admitted what I was doing and she saw the results. I felt like a mad scientist or a back-alley doctor when I was enhancing friends' photos with my self-taught skills, charging people mates' rates for a dodgy underground service. Gwen would slide her USB stick under the desk in my parents' office like we were smuggling illegal drugs. Her picture would load up slowly onto the screen, her long thick hair flowing around her face, the tiniest blemishes visible around her chin and in front of her ears. She wasn't spotty, but her skin was uneven in places and usually a few different shades (like any other human being on earth). I mean, we were normal-looking teenagers; it wasn't rocket science that we weren't quite ready to grace the cover of a magazine. But we still felt compelled to try to compete as best we could. It was a strange point to be at as a teen: insecure enough to need to edit ourselves heavily but smug enough to be clued up on exactly what these magazines were doing to women's bodies and faces. We were simply playing them at their own game.

Gwen would smile and nod as I painted away her blemishes and dark circles. A few moments later her eyes would sparkle as she saw her face transform into a slightly smoother version of herself. I was addicted to the reaction we'd both get. It was like I was the host of *Changing Rooms* or *Ground Force*, sliding open the curtains for the 'big reveal' and hearing the client gasp with delight, screaming: 'OH MY GOD I LOVE IT!' We'd bond over how perfect I could make her look on the screen and she'd always leave my house one happy customer.

The reason we were obsessed with getting the right photo of ourselves was because that year we'd discovered MSN Messenger. Downloading MSN for the first time, especially on a school computer, felt rebellious and exciting. It soon became the microcosm of our entire social lives. In that heated online environment we were constantly building and destroying friendships; things had the power to make or break you, so it was wise to at least give yourself a head start with a nice photo. It was our way of feeling as though we were armouring ourselves before going into the online battlefield.

There was a square box to the right of the messaging bar where you were meant to upload a picture of yourself. This was important to get right, because socialising with the opposite sex was not a frequent occurrence in my life at this point, so this really was the only way anyone could work out what someone looked liked before attempting to awkwardly flirt. This was before the days of Facebook stalking or even proper Googling, so all we had to go off was that one photo to see if someone might be worth turning into a romantic suitor. (Yes, I know what you're thinking: heartlessly judging someone by just one glimpse of a tiny photo – sounds familiar? Well, we were doing this way before Tinder.) The idea of a 'profile picture' was new to us: *which one should we choose; what impression do we want people to have; should we go for innocent, sexy or intellectual; who are we, really?* Little did we know, this was our very first foray into the notion of 'selling ourselves' online and building up an 'online presence'.

We now know, especially since the birth of dating apps, that one picture (or even three) doesn't always paint an honest one. I looked different in *all* my pictures, mainly because I was a Photoshop Addict but also because I was a teenager, frequently changing hairstyles and body size, and conducting strange sartorial experiments. Sometimes, due to my varying hormones, I'd feel like a completely different person every day. It was a hard task to pick a photo that I could feel confident about but which was authentic enough that it wouldn't totally freak people out or make me completely unrecognisable IRL. (The biggest compliment I get, even to this day, is: 'Emma! Hi! It's [@name] from Twitter, I'm surprised, you *actually* look a bit like your profile pic!')

One photo was all it took to imagine a person as my spouse. My head was full of daydreams about boys who I'd met in IRL for ten minutes outside of the school gate, as they awkwardly hunched over me with their rucksacks and pigeon-toed feet, but who seemed much cooler over the Internet. My imagination would go wild; I'd decide I fancied someone from their one profile picture and from there I would dream up ideas of what they would be like in a relationship. It was a superpower that I think all teenage girls use – the ability to daydream and imagine conversations and relationships, and fantasise to the point where you actually feel for a few seconds it might be true. In those days I had long-term relationships with many different boys, including celebrities, inside my own head, some of which I can still remember now because they seemed so real at the time. It was similar to when you dream about someone and it's so vivid that you end up hating them for a few days in real life because they did something awful in the dream. These intense daydreams normally happened when I was away with my parents on holiday, headphones in, sun on my face, whispering Incubus lyrics and imagining relationships with boys I knew nothing about and had met only for five minutes. Not having a smartphone meant a lot of daydreaming. And why not? They were perfect in my head. But this was the problem: they were great inside my mind and on the Internet, but absolute shit-bags in real life.

Still, I didn't know that at the time and so that square little box was important to me because it would occasionally help me move an Internet relationship into a Real-Life Date. A lucky few girls from the classroom had been selected before for a Real-Life Date and the rest of us would pretend we weren't fussed while trying to hide a deep, hot furnace of jealousy burning inside. It reminded me of that tragic scene in *Grease* at the school dance where the 'benched' girls are sitting around the edge of the dance floor, clicking their heels, hoping that someone would choose them to have a dance, as Danny Zuko and Cha Cha glide across the dance floor, hand in hand, sliding right past all the desperate ones. But there we were: a group of teenage girls waiting to be 'chosen' from behind the MSN Messenger screen.

Obviously, it wasn't all about romance; we would also anxiously wait to be asked on friend dates too. I'd get just as nervous when the Queen Bee of the classroom would pop up online and would desperately wait for her to pick me as her New Best Friend. It was the basic need to feel accepted high up in the social chain. I was nervous every time I logged into MSN, because after a while I would always be able to suss out who liked me, who didn't and who was pretending to. I wanted the boys to fancy me and I wanted the cool girls to be my friends, and on MSN it was always one step forward, two steps back. Worming your way into the cool kids MSN group-chats wasn't easy. It was exhausting trying to keep everyone's attention, without being the centre of a school scandal.

As a result, I became more and more transfixed on making my online self look a certain way. By a 'certain way' I mean more desirable in the context of what I thought society wanted. It started with the airbrushing of my face, the brightening of my eyes, the saturation of my skin. Later, when I discovered Myspace, I became obsessed with adding volume to my hair and chopping off bits of my waist like a sushi chef. I started to become lazy with what I was wearing and relaxed with the outcome of photos because I could always *fix it online later.*

A few years later, in 2006 when I was still in school, I joined Facebook for the first time. In those days, it was all about 1) pretending you were a university student so you could cheat the sign-up system, and 2) writing utter drivel on anyone and everyone's wall, and not much else. (There were some Myspace hangers on who didn't trust my foray into the land of Facebook but they later succumbed. Lots of people signed up to FaceBox by accident, a website that shortly afterwards died a lonely death.) Then, a little while after, Facebook introduced photo-uploading, aka photo albums, and we started to get inundated with up to sixty pictures of someone's 'random night out'. It was the first time we could properly share lots of different pictures at once and not have to just depend on that little MSN profile picture to spell out the story of our lives.

Photo-sharing is so normal now that it is totally crazy to remember that this was a relatively 'new thing' only ten years ago. We've also become more selective as the years have gone on, thank God. What essentially happened is that we were invited to 'share' for the first time, and humans, as we know, LOVE to share, so we all went for it at 100mph. Even if I just had some pictures of the back of someone's head in a nightclub, it was going up online the next day. The more you uploaded, the more you felt part of the tribe. It made you feel more secure in your circle of friends. So it was no wonder I wanted to edit them to within an inch of their life to present my best self to my social group. Documenting our lives in such minute detail felt like it was bringing us closer together in some way. We were so public with everything, including writing long essays on each other's walls. Now we can see the shift, we are so much more selective with what we upload, sharing one perfect Instagram instead of uploading fifty photos from our camera roll to an online album.

The secrecy involved in editing my photos before uploading them on Facebook felt like the short period in which I had attempted bulimia. Editing my body and purging my food both made me feel thin. Of course, I had to cover up my tracks in both cases, but these methods allowed me to look slim and still eat as much as I wanted. This was a win-win, surely.

However, a few years later something began to change. Keeping up online appearances was exhausting and I never felt like myself.

I remember one time where I'd gone too far. I uploaded an album called 'Portugal Snaps' and my friends were slightly confused.

'Em, you look *thinner*?' they accused, as they clicked through them on the school computer, mouths hanging slightly open. 'What did you *do*?'

'I just retouched them a little bit,' I said, chewing obnoxiously on a Cheestring.

'What? You can't do that!'

They were scrolling through the comments on each photo, watching as they came in thick and fast from random people at the surrounding schools. 'Gorgeous!' read one. 'Skinny minny!' read another. 'Jealous of your body!' read another.

I was lapping it up, ignoring the confusion and thinking it was genius that I could look great in digital. Deep down, though, I could see how my friends were struggling to be relaxed about it. I'd gone too far. Now I know what they must have been thinking: I'd created, or should I say Photoshopped, a monster. A monster with great thighs and flawless skin. Receiving endless compliments for something that wasn't real was stirring up some very unsettling feelings. This wasn't a cute case of 'imposter syndrome', believing I wasn't as attractive in real life as I actually was; I had been an *actual* imposter online for almost that full year. I wondered if it was too late to change my ways. What would my Facebook friends say? Would they notice? Would they reject the real me?

The answer was 'no – don't be ridiculous'. The funniest thing in all of this is that, apart from the close friends who had called me out on the Portugal photo album, no one else had noticed my Photoshop addiction. And after I started reining in the retouching and hesitantly posting the resulting natural photos, *no one* noticed that I no longer had a Photoshopped thigh gap. No one cared about the huge zit in the middle of my nose. No one was printing out before and after photos and calling me up on it. Because, guess what, people are too busy looking at their own profiles and their own pictures to truly care about yours. No one cares more than you about your own social media profiles. While you are doing you, everyone else is doing them. If anything, I had better banter in my comments section and I felt like me. Albeit I felt like a fool for having pretended for so long.

Over the years, something inside of me became more relaxed and less uptight about how I look in photos, and in real life. I began to cringe at my shiny Photoshopped face. I started to feel relieved to be myself and to truly relax into my own body. I was coming out of angsty teenage years and beginning to understand why I was feeling the way I felt, and why I felt the need to look a certain way. As I began to read more, I became less obsessed with Pritt-Sticking perfect-looking girls into my diary and circling them with bubble-writing saying: 'I WISH I LOOKED LIKE THIS.' I was growing up, and I was reading and watching women whose worth was defined by so much more than the definition of their abs, or the whiteness of their teeth or the smoothness of their skin. I was starting to understand that my need for perfection – which was so laughably out of reach anyway that I can't believe I'd wasted so much time on it – was not actually my fault. It was the fault of centuries of people telling women that they need to be pretty little objects and looking a certain way was the fastest, most failsafe way to achieve 'success'.

But my real 'lightbulb moment' happened during an awkward encounter at a squash lesson (I was really into my racquet sports at this age). A guy came up to me and asked me why I was wearing so much make-up to play sport in. I felt really embarrassed. I couldn't win. I was being told constantly through my exposure to magazines and advertising that women need to slap on the make-up to feel like human beings and yet here I was also being scolded for wearing too much of it. I just felt like I had to be a million different things to live up to everyone's different expectations and there was no way I could ever achieve any of them.

From there it was a short step to getting angry. I thought to myself: what if I can't actually win? What if the only answer in all of this is to just be myself without changing anything on the outside? Actually, it went something like this: FUCK THIS! I'M TIRED OF PRETENDING! And I'm lucky that my body works! Why don't I experiment with being happy with what I've got? Why haven't I tried that yet? Why should I feel I have to crop bits out of my own image, leaving it looking like an incomplete puzzle?

In other words, this was my 'I'm gonna let my freak flag fly!' moment – and it felt amazing.

Of course, technology has evolved since my dodgy Microsoft Paint episodes and so has our addiction to presenting the best versions of ourselves. It's easier than ever to crop, edit, filter and fill in our personal photos before we share them with the world. Even Brooklyn Beckham was filmed by *Miss Vogue* to give his guide to Instagram. The main takeaways were: don't use a selfie stick and make sure your feed is not just full of your own face.

Recently, a YouTube video on 'how to edit your Instagram photos' went viral within the media community. The reaction was huge: do people really edit their photos in that minute detail? REALLY? Have we been believing 'real' people's social media pictures when in fact they're no different to any mainstream fashion magazine's Photoshopped and professionally lit images? It was clear that the YouTuber was confessing to having a proper *process* to achieve perfection. She walked us through her movements step by step, she showed us the many apps that she uses to get her photos just right, and to keep them all consistently beautiful on her feed. She told us she uses the 'refine' tool of Facetune to edit a strand of hair. A strand. As you can probably guess, the photo in my eyes looked already perfect to me. She then plumped up pieces of hair by dragging them outwards with her finger. She smoothed down the ridge of her nose. Next, she opened up the Faded or VSCO Cam app. She changed the exposure and saturation of the photo – 'but not too orangey'. Then on to the PicFrame app, to pick the perfect border. It was astonishing how many apps were being used to craft this one perfect photo. There's not a lot of difference between this and an airbrushed version of a mega Hollywood actress on the cover of *Cosmopolitan* magazine. The only difference is that this blogger was being *honest* about it – but she was still doing it and perpetuating the idea that it's okay – and even desirable – to post images that are very far away from their original state.

This blogger isn't the only one doing it, of course. When I type in 'selfie photo editing tool' I get 5,480,000 search results staring back at me. I know another blogger, I'll call her V, who admits she uses an app to add make-up to her face so that she can post a selfie without opening her physical make-up bag or stepping outside.

Is it ironic then, that while it seems we all edit our Instagram images, Julia Robert's L'Oréal advert was pulled by the Advertising Standards Authority in 2011 because it was misrepresentative of the product, suggesting that something concrete is finally being done about Photoshopping in adverts. Fast-forward a few years, and Julia Roberts posted a no make-up selfie on Instagram in 2015 with the caption: 'We overlay our faces with tons of make-up. We get Botox and even starve ourselves to become that perfect size. We try to fix something but you can't fix what you can't see. It's the soul that needs the surgery. It's time that we take a stand.' Social media can be used for good when people choose to engage with it positively.

In 2002, the legendary Jamie Lee Curtis also took a stand against editing and posed for *More* magazine make-up-free and untouched. Her reasoning was this: 'I don't have great thighs. I have very big breasts and a soft, fatty little tummy. And I've got back fat. People assume that I'm walking around in little spaghetti-strap dresses. It's insidious – Glam Jamie, the Perfect Jamie, the great figure, blah, blah, blah. And I don't want the unsuspecting forty-year-old women of the world to think that I've got it going on. It's such a fraud. And I'm the one perpetuating it.'

This made me reflect on my own behaviour and how everyone has an element of responsibility not to perpetuate things that aren't real. No one can show 100 per cent of their life, in most cases we only see the showreel. That's a lot of time spent imagining someone's life and tricking people into believing it's better than it is.

I've always been grateful for the people who show the 'bloopers' of their life. One good thing about social media is that – in its best aspect – it can be a platform for authenticity, for example when we see people like Cara Delevingne uploading Dubmash videos of herself singing along with her mates. On social media, Christine Teigen shared a photo of herself on the sofa with her dog because she doesn't like sleeping in the bed when her husband, John Legend, is away. The Beckhams show us their family holiday snaps. Lena Dunham uses Instagram to challenge stereotypes from weight to abortions to mental health to endometriosis. YouTubers like Zoella vlog without make-up and discuss the inner details of her panic attacks. This means celebrities have, for the first time, been able to give more of an unfiltered insight into their lives. We find out more about who they really are. They can directly slam down tabloid rumours.

On the flipside, we now see people – non-celebrities – around us using editing tools to Photoshop every aspect of their life. I know a handful of popular bloggers who admit to editing photos of their breakfasts, who lay things out on Instagram like a professional food stylist. Why are we so scared to show real photos of real things?

Even on Facebook we have the ability to ask someone to remove a bad picture of us, curating a more 'perfect' personal environment. It's not *editing*, it's removing an image entirely. To do this you have to construct a bit of an awkward plea email, which is automated by Facebook: 'Hi [insert name who uploaded the shit photo of you], I really don't like this picture of me. Please can you take it down?' You then wait anxiously, hoping no one has seen the incriminating image and that the person you've messaged will take pity on you for looking like your fictional and unfortunate twin sister. This is a way of editing out bad stuff, much like I used to edit out a bad zit.

All this new technology at our disposal makes us think we are in control of what is shown of us online, even if we are not really. Facebook wants us to *feel* like we're in control. It's all part of the magic trick. You feel safe on a platform surrounded by all your friends, oversharing every aspect of your life, with all your data being scraped by little robots behind the scenes who can then sell you things that they know you like.

The option to remove parts of our lives online also shows that we are increasingly worried about our online personas. The rise of Snapchat shows we actually quite like a platform deleting stuff for us. But is it healthy for us to constantly survey which of our photos are 'bad', or not 100 per cent perfect? Is it a positive thing that we are in some control of our own image or worrying that we feel the need to cut out the 'real' bits of our lives if they show us in a less-than-perfect light?

Moderating our lives too closely can be dangerously addictive. Should we strive to embrace our facial defects or quirks and bad photos because they are part of us? Should we just learn to love all of our angles and all our imperfections? Shouldn't we just shake what we've got and be proud of every tagged photo? Or do we deserve to have a bit of control over what is shown of our faces online, without feeling ashamed of ourselves either?

Recently, my heart fell into my lap on receiving a press release from the Dove Self-Esteem Project that said that the 'average UK girl takes twelve minutes to prepare for a single "selfie", thus spending eighty-four minutes a week getting ready for selfies'. That's a whole lot of time that could be used for something else. All that time is being spent on clambering to receive the queen of external validation: the 'Like'.

How far is too far when it comes to making ourselves camera-ready at all times? What about when selfie anxiety drives you to make dramatic decisions that change your looks permanently? Dr Alan Matarasso, an upmarket American plastic surgeon, said in the *New York Times* that 'social media is having a massive impact' on people requesting surgery. 'It has opened up plastic surgery to a whole new segment of potential patients. People are walking around with cameras 24/7. They get a lip injection and one minute later they are on Instagram showing off their new look.'

I don't want to get to a place where we don't look like us and our friends don't look like our friends.

Of course, it's possible to take nice photos without the need to edit the shit out of all of them. And it can be a positive thing to do so. If I'm having a terrific outfit/make-up day I will happily take a load of selfies. I feel like we should document the times we know we're having a good day. So when people say to me or about me,

'God, she must love herself, she takes so many selfies,' my response is always: 'Damn right I love myself.' I spent years hating my looks and editing out chunks of my face and thighs and arse. Thanks for checking in, though! The problem isn't girls thinking they look nice in selfies, the problem is the girls who don't think they are pretty enough to take any. So let's all #GoTakeASelfie and like like like it.

I now urge myself and others to appreciate what they have. When I was hunched over my huge PC editing my body as a young teenager, I actually looked good. The irony! Of course I did, I was young; my skin was way better than it is now. Nothing was as *awful* as I thought it was. I definitely wish I had spent more time playing in the garden during those years than being hunched over my computer using editing tools, trying desperately to enhance a digital version of me. What a waste of time and energy. I'm glad I realised before it was too late.

Be more like Olive in *Little Miss Sunshine* and you can't go wrong. Get out there in the world, warts and all. You don't get the time back.

'It's the new frontier of misogyny – take a woman who's in control of her life and then silence her.'

Hannah Horvath, Girls

chapter 2

I Discover Cybersex

2003

'Turn on your webcam.'

A little message popped up on CyberChat, a pixelated chat room that made the noise of an arcade machine whenever anyone signed in. I had logged into this rebellious online destination for the third time in a day, getting increasingly addicted to – and excited by – who and what I might find. I was hooked on this dangerous little website that allowed anyone, of any age, to sign in and start conversations with total strangers. Not an 'I've already looked you up on LinkedIn and you look respectable from your haircut' type of stranger – no, an actual silhouetted stranger. You never had any idea who you were talking to as the profile picture for each user was too tiny and blurry, but that was where the excitement came from. I could offload the weirdest stuff in my brain to someone who I would never meet. Essentially, to me, it was free therapy. It was thrilling, entertaining and a bit rebellious.

Sometimes I'd have friends round for a group sleepover, and instead of watching TV we'd all sit on beanbags and then squish ourselves around the computer with a glass of Ribena, ready to have a laugh with strangers and trick them into thinking we fancied them or let them tell us rude things that made us giggle and that we would later repress. We'd ask for these men to put on their webcam and would then type 'Show us your willy!' – only to quickly log off as we saw a belt being unfastened, screeching as we scrambled to click the 'X' in the corner of the screen like we were frantically trying to find the exit in the London Dungeons. It fast became our favourite indoor hobby. Other times we'd go at it alone and privately start experimenting with different parts of our personality, being whoever we wanted to be with nobody else interfering. We treated it like a game, with no real consequences.

This time I was alone.

'I said, turn on your webcam.'

My parents were out of the house for a few hours but my grandparents were keeping an eye on me next door. I say 'keeping an eye on me' but they definitely didn't know enough about computers to police any behaviour; they had no idea what I was doing on there, it was totally alien to them. Technology is such an easy thing to sneak around on, to hide from people who know less than you – I would hear them coming and just press the space bar until the conversation was hidden.

I was in my Snoopy pyjamas and chatting to a sixteen-year-old boy called Ben who said he lived in Cornwall and attended a school that I'd vaguely heard of. I don't know how I first stumbled across him, but when I searched for strangers to talk to, the results were displayed by location so I could see where any 'chat friend' was based. I was in Devon. I decided to be strategic in who I picked to talk to; making sure they weren't too close to where I lived (just in case they turned out to be a mass murderer) but close enough so that if we got on, and potentially fell madly in love, it wouldn't be impossible to meet up one day. I had read the horror stories; I wasn't about to meet with anyone in real life any time soon, especially without finding out a bit more information first.

When it came to Ben, though, I couldn't help but keep my fingers crossed that he was who he said he was. He'd sent me a picture a few days prior: a young tanned blond boy carrying a surfboard with extremely toned arms. But I knew anyone could fake a picture. He looked outdoorsy and had a good smile. I gave myself a virtual pat on the back. This was fourteen-year-old me's type. An incredibly inoffensive sporty type. Disgustingly Disney. We had been chatting with each other via MSN and texting for nearly a month.

Right now, however, he was asking to see me and I was freaking out. I'd been brave enough to tell him in passing that my mum had bought a webcam for the family computer but didn't expect him to be so persistent with wanting me to turn it on. I had wet hair from just getting out of the bath, and was wearing a pink fluffy dressing gown, curled up on my parents' big desk chair listening to Panic at the Disco and painting my nails silver. I didn't feel prepared for Ben to see me like this. After all, what if he didn't like what he saw? My hands were getting clammy just thinking about it. It was the same feeling I'd get before going on stage in the school play. Waiting in the wings. Legs wobbling, palms getting sticky.

But he wouldn't stop asking, so I quickly went to the bathroom mirror to put concealer under my eyes and pat down my hair. My thinking was that if Ben saw me like this maybe he'd be pleasantly surprised when tomorrow I turned on the webcam having made a proper effort, sampling some of the blue hair mascara that I got for my birthday. So I turned it on quickly, sitting in front of it as I fiddled awkwardly with the Post-it notes left on Mum's desk, waiting for him to comment on my appearance. The webcam stayed switched on for ten minutes, which felt like an eternity, but Ben seemed to have disappeared. I realised his status said 'Away' on our chat screen. It was 19.03 and Ben had last typed something at 18.41. It was unlike him to just leave his computer without telling me. So I yanked the webcam lead off of the top of the family computer and the connection suddenly went blank.

'Hey – I'd turned it on! Did you see me? Something's gone wrong now though … I can't turn it back on,' I lied.

I tried to act relaxed but I was so desperate for his approval.

No reply. I waited another five minutes.

'Ben?'

Another minute.

'You there???'

I went to get a glass of water to pass the time. This was the first time I felt an overwhelming anxiety from the Internet. The idea that you could put yourself out there and you could be rejected as a result made me feel so small, and stupid for trying. In hindsight, I was putting myself up for approval from a stranger. I was essentially giving a virtual person, through a machine, permission to have a positive or negative effect on my real-life emotions. Getting a flirty text from Ben would be the making of my mood, good or bad. My family would find my behaviour totally unpredictable, and they had no idea where my highs and lows were coming from. And how could they? Neither did I. A teenager's moods aren't only dictated by hormones but also a hundred possible external variables. Mine were being dictated by one thing only: Ben's messages.

It was sad, but true.

I went back to the computer, praying to have heard back from him. And I had:

'Yo. Sorry. God you are amazing. I had to go and sort myself out if you know what I mean ;)'

I actually didn't know what he meant. I was fourteen.

'I had to bash one out.'

My reaction was to freeze like a rabbit in the headlights, hands hovering over my keyboard in mid-air, not having a clue what to say. This guy had just admitted to getting so turned on by me in my dressing gown that he went and had a wank for half an hour in the toilet. I felt sick to the stomach and started to panic that I might not be able to get out of this situation. But was it weird that I was kind of flattered? And, hang on – what if he knew where I lived? What if he was a stalker with a gun? What if my parents found out? I didn't think this was normal. And more to the point: when was I going to get a chance to see *him* to check he was who he said he was? Surely he owed it to me now? Who was I actually talking to? Was I going to be murdered?

'Is your webcam working yet?' I asked, rather politely in the circumstances. Inside my heart was racing.

'Come back online at 9 p.m., I'll put it on then.'

I had a few hours to kill before I could find out the cold hard truth about the person I'd been talking to online for the best part of a month, every night, growing more and more attached to the *idea* of him. I went and watched TV for a couple of hours, catching up on episodes of *Saved by the Bell*, daydreaming of Ben, wondering if he'd look as attractive as he did in his photo or whether I was about to find out that Ben was a sixty-three-year-old Russian woman. Nervously fidgeting on the sofa, I tried to relax and not flinch every time my phone screen lit up. My Nokia 3210 was on the table,staring at me with its pixelated numbers spelling out the time. He'd often text me if we weren't chatting online, but I hadn't heard anything and I was getting tetchy. Time slowly ticked by and eventually it was only half an hour to wait until 9 p.m. I started to change the settings on my Nokia from silent (I didn't want to know if he'd texted me) to loud (I wanted to know immediately if he'd texted me) and continued doing this until I realised how ridiculous I was being. Eventually, I just shoved my phone under a cushion on the sofa out of frustration. I always enjoy seeing those montages in Hollywood films when the girl is waiting for a text and a cheesy song is playing while the protagonist stares at their phone as they clean their teeth, or the phone's in viewing distance from the shower, or next to them on the loo. That was exactly what I was doing. I then went upstairs and lay on my bed listening to Avril Lavigne: she summed up my antisocial emotions perfectly. *Complicated.*

At 8.59 p.m. I scrambled to the computer room and it took about fifteen minutes to even turn the computer back on, connect the dial-up Internet and check my parents weren't using the home phone. I logged back on and could see that Ben was online. My tummy did a little flip as it normally did when I saw his MSN name.

Ben: Hey you

Emma: HI! You OK?

B: Yep yep … OK you ready to see me? ;)

E: Yes … of course ;) My cam's still broke :(but I wanna see YOU!

I felt knots of nerves tighten in my stomach. Oh God, please look like your photo. Please. Please.

B: OK … One tic … just putting it on now …

The chat-room window suddenly came alive, with a moving image of Ben in the top right-hand corner of our chat screen. I expanded the webcam pop-up so it took up the entire screen, and made sure the computer room door was firmly shut, so that my little sister couldn't charge in and shout at me for something I didn't do. His voice echoed throughout the small room, at least he *sounds* sixteen, I thought. I quickly turned down the volume, and when I looked back up I was mind-blown. He was who he said he was. He had blond hair swept to one side with a bit of gel, just like the picture, and he was wearing no top, his shoulders glistening in the light. There was a dimple on one side of his face (and in his chin) and he had extremely shiny teeth. He was breathtaking. He stood up and I saw his boxer shorts. This guy was unreal. And he knew it. I smirked. He smirked.

At first, obviously I was just relieved that Ben hadn't been lying to me. I'd become suspicious after he started to encourage me on the first night we'd chatted to start sexting. I didn't want to sex text anyone until I knew exactly who I was talking to. But now that I could see he was who he said he was I decided this was my chance to experiment. I wasn't afraid to up my game. He was basically a blond Jonas brother, with or without the purity ring. We chatted back and forth for a few hours before my Internet stopped working. So I went upstairs, climbed into bed and immediately texted him:

Emma: Seeing you today … it's made me horny!
Ben: Me too. What things would you do to me? ;)

E: Um, I would hold your…you know…

B: Then what?

E: Kiss you. Slide my vagina up and down your leg.

B: What else?

Ben kept prompting me to continue.

On and on I went. I was absolutely clueless and didn't care about how anything sounded. I was free-styling with my language, adding in random bits of the human anatomy here and there, saying the sort of stuff that I guessed boys would want to hear; totally making it up as I went along. I stole one-liners from adult films I'd secretly watched and the sex columns in *J-17* magazine that I used to steal from my babysitter (each time she'd buy it I'd steal it and hide it down the back of the bathroom unit and then fish it out when she wasn't looking. Poor woman, she must have been so confused). I also threw in to my sex-text chat the stuff my dirtiest friends at school had shown me on their phones, all the shorthand and abbreviated lingo for sex positions. I had one friend in particular who treated sex research like her favourite hobby. She was constantly getting out sex books and then sharing the gory details with us, and telling us all the stuff she'd done on her 'holiday flings'. Her attitude to being herself and enjoying researching sex in such detail at the age of fourteen was to be admired, even though it totally freaked me out at the time.

As for me, I was only telling Ben things that maybe I wouldn't actually be afraid to 'try' in real life one day. I was experimenting with what I enjoyed saying, and what he responded well to. I would hide my phone under my pillow each time I pressed send to pretend for a moment I hadn't written what I'd just written. But I enjoyed the I-can't-believe-I-just-said-that thrill of it all. And it kept progressing, until I was basically having no-holds-barred cybersex with him. Who knew whether or not I was saying or doing the right things, but it felt exciting – and more importantly, virtual. I was only brave enough to say these things from behind a screen. There was no way I actually wanted to do the real thing. I was using the Internet to experiment with what I did or didn't physically want to do. For now, I didn't even need to worry about doing it in real life, I could fantasise and discuss anything and everything without leaving the safety of my home-slash-bed. I was pushing my limits and putting the wildest suggestions out there, all from behind a screen.

That night I had an orgasm for the first time. It was sort of a blurry daydream, as I worked out that I could control this virtual reality inside my head, neatly compiling my different fantasies. This was the first time I realised just how much female orgasms relied on the mind, as well as the body. Ben kind of looked a bit like my current TV obsession (a younger version of Ryan from *The OC*, who coincidentally is called Ben in real life. *OC* fans, only you can appreciate that) so I managed to blur the two boys into one and imagined up a romantic sex dream. I let a wave of sensations ripple through me, from my lower body up to my head, which gave me a head rush that seemed to last for about ten minutes; I was hot in the face and warm all over. Afterwards I couldn't stop thinking about Ben and re-reading our text conversation over and over. It felt so rebellious; intimate; private. All taking place from the confines of my single bed. I slept well that night.

The next day at school, I felt different. Even my walk was slightly different, slightly more confident: more Spice Girl, less fourteen-year-old virgin. I swanned into my classroom and smiled as I emptied my books into my desk, looking around trying to conceal my smug expression. It was like the feeling of wearing a matching bra and pants: only you know about it, and you can't help but feel great, even if no one else knows the reason why.

As with all schools, the hierarchy between us girls was always very clear. I was floating in the middle, equidistant to the 'cool kids' and the 'losers'. These so-called 'losers' didn't give a crap about following the trends or sucking up to people. The 'cool kids', I later learned, wouldn't necessarily be the cool adults. They would get complacent; they would peak too early, and be surprised when stuff wasn't handed to them on a plate. You can tell who was a previous cool kid when they were younger because they will still reminisce about school way into their late twenties or early thirties, while everyone else doesn't want to bring it up, ever. I felt like I had just as much in common with both: like the cool kids I was a big attention seeker and could be rude and awful to teachers, but like the losers I didn't fit in with anyone and I wasn't exactly aesthetically pleasing with my greasy ponytail and huge metal braces.

Lucy, the girl at the top of the food chain, made a beeline for me that Monday morning. She sashayed towards me in her rolled-up kilted skirt with her tanned, long legs. She was the first and only girl at school who had starting shaving her legs. We would stare at her hairless knees.

'I hear you're talking to a guy called Ben at the moment.' Lucy chewed bubblegum quite loudly in between her words. She must have heard this information from the handful of people I confided in. This proved yet again I couldn't trust anyone by saying 'please don't tell anyone'. Whatever I'd written on MSN had probably already been copied and pasted into at least seven other conversations.

The penny dropped for the first time: the Internet was a much quicker way to spread gossip.

'Er … yes. He is called Ben, yes. How do you—' I didn't expect anyone to actually *know* Ben. I'd met him through a random chat-room algorithm. It wasn't possible.

'Well, I used to go to school with him, when I lived in Cornwall. We went out for a bit.' She popped her bubblegum a bit too close to my face. She looked me up and down. 'He's cool.'

I felt sick. I didn't like the fact that my private online sext buddy had history or any connections to my daily life. *That wasn't supposed to happen.* Especially with someone like Lucy, who was a talker and a big fish in a small pond. I wondered if they were still in touch. Or how he could have been with her and then gone for someone like me. My chest felt tight, but I decided to just shrug it off, and pretend it was nothing. He was just a guy I spoke to sometimes. Nothing major. Nothing to see here. But it was obvious she knew something I didn't. I could see it in her evil eyeliner-heavy eyes.

I went about my day, trying not to be paranoid. Double geography (*yawn*); followed by drama (my favourite lesson, getting lost in other people's lives); then maths (the lesson I was 90 per cent likely to get told off in for being an 'annoying' distraction. I still like to believe that I didn't talk the *most*, I just had the most distinctive *voice*, which I would go on to realise is a positive thing when trying to get someone's attention in a business meeting). Then it was lunch break, and I discovered Lucy sitting on her desk with Rosie and Laura, her two cartoonish sidekicks, huddled together like evil penguins. They were giggling about something on their phone.

One of my close friends, Ellie, the classroom peacemaker, leaned in towards me as I went over to sit next to her. She didn't beat around the bush.

'Em, I think Lucy knows something you don't about that guy you've been talking to. I don't know what, but I heard her discussing it earlier with the gruesome twosome. You should try and find out.'

Ellie had a heart of gold, and if something didn't sit right with her, she found a way to break news gently to people, never stirring, just gently sharing vital information that could save a lot of tears later down the line. Her style was to whisper some intel into your ear and then disappear off like a peacemaking butterfly into the playground.

The lunch bell rang, and Rosie and Laura peeled away from Lucy, leaving her on her own momentarily. She was crunching into an apple with attitude. I braved it and went over, because not knowing was making me feel sicker than the thought of actually confronting her and finding out what she knew. I suddenly imagined everyone knowing something I didn't, like that feeling I'd often get when I'd have an anxious dream about coming into school totally naked or having lost all of my front teeth. I calmly asked her what she was talking about earlier and if there was anything I should know.

Her answer was abrupt: 'K, I'll tell you tonight on MSN.'

Seldom were things as bad as someone saying 'K' to you.

This was the downside of the Internet at this age: things were used against you behind your back, rumours would circulate online and information could be kept from you until the evenings when the gossip would come to a head as you'd log on. The post-6 p.m. 'after-school' Internet session was something to look forward to and dread in equal measure, because it was a little elite group who joined in: the ones at school whose parents had a computer, and were 'cool' enough to stay up past bedtime and go online late at night. If you didn't have an Internet connection, or had strict parents, it meant you were ostracised from most of the gossip and inside information. Feeling left out of 'private jokes' and 'in-chat' at school was horrible. You'd be sitting on the periphery, not able to join in or laugh at what everyone else was laughing at. You'd worry they might be laughing about you. The worst thing at school was feeling like you didn't fit in. And the Internet only heightened these feelings. You were either in on the joke, or you were the joke.

So I had no choice but to wait. The bullies were skilled in making me feel vulnerable in real life so that I'd have to hang on until later that evening to log on nervously and find out what people had been saying. It could turn into a mean game. Having other people in control of how your friends might perceive you is the most crushing thing, especially at fourteen. I'd have to ask my mum nicely to use the computer. But I didn't want her knowing that I might be on the receiving end of a bullying tactic so I tried not to act too desperate to get online. I just prayed that she didn't know what I was doing on the computer or see the conversations. I have a feeling she did, though. It was easy to look up MSN conversations and my mum admitted, a few years later, to finding some of my saved MSN files, which mortified me.

After school that night I waited for Lucy to come online. Her MSN name was ~QUEEN-BEE~ which was obviously terrifying. At 7.23 p.m. I heard the ping, and there she was. She took ages to reply to me when I made contact; probably revelling in the power games she was playing, while all the time knots were tightening in my stomach. To be able to see that someone 'is typing' can just be the most nerve-inducing thing. I couldn't handle the wait. I'm impatient. I'm a Gemini.

'Hi. Sorry I didn't tell you at school today. But thought you should know.'

She then copied and pasted a link.

I clicked it immediately and held my breath as it opened, buffering slowly because of our stressfully slow home Internet connection.

It had loaded. Ben had made a public thread on an Internet forum called 'Emma's Cyber Sexting!' And there it was. Word for word, all of my incriminating text messages publicly posted. In many different comments underneath the main profile he'd clearly manually typed out all of the stuff I'd texted or messaged him over the course of the previous few weeks. It included a photo he'd taken surreptitiously of me in my dressing gown with wet hair through my webcam.

I felt so violated, so tricked, like he'd come in and stolen something from me. When, how, why? I'd noticed, the slimy rat, that he'd actually never really said much to me in response in our text conversations; he'd always just prompted me to get more into the conversation and expose more of my sexual feelings towards him – clearly, so he could use it in this twisted forum. How could I have been so naive? I felt like Drew Barrymore in *Never Been Kissed*, at that bit in the film when her date rocks up and instead of greeting her at the door, he laughs and throws eggs at her from out of his car sunroof. So hopeful, so *humiliated*. So unaware.

There was comment after comment. I scrolled through the entire never-ending website page. It was mostly boys ripping apart my 'sexy conversation', laughing and shrieking at my use of words, my fantasies, my obsessions that I'd told Ben in private (or so I thought). He was having a laugh about it, but instead of inviting his friends over for a private giggle, he'd decided to publicly shame me, for all to see.

One of the messages read:

LOL This is so fucking embarrassing. Has this girl even had sex before? OH GOD. Wouldn't go near her.

Another read:

TRAGIC SEX CHAT! HAHAHA. She's got a lot to learn!

Another:

She needs a good seeing to! LOL

I was fourteen, so I doubt my 'peers' knew much in the sex department either. I'd had my first experience of being Internet shamed and bullied by teenage boys. It was fine for Ben to have written rude things involving his penis, but me? A girl sharing intimate thoughts about masturbation and her vagina? Utterly shocking, totally laughable. Apparently. Kind of troll-worthy, even.

It's over a decade later and I still see Ben pop up online when I least expect it. And still, even though I am now a proper adult (with a mortgage and everything), it gives me a faded memory of anxiety. That's another thing about the Internet: your past can come back and haunt you at any time when you least expect it, even when your life is going swimmingly. Although the old Myspace profiles are hidden in the depths of Google and my old Bebo profiles dead and buried, everything is re-discoverable. At least, anything can be a reminder. The permanency of the Internet can be a good and bad thing. Bad if you've been Internet shamed and you want it to go away, good if there's a great profile picture of you on the first page of Google Images.

I was searching for an old email from a friend also called Ben and loads of these decade-old flirty emails appeared from Sex Texter Ben (yes, I still use my old email address occasionally as my 'spam bin'). It's weird when you're in Adult World and then suddenly you're faced with a blast from the Ghost of Teenage Anxiety Past. I started reading them (I'm only human) and gasped at the horror. My eyes widened as I kept scrolling, going deeper into the memories of my old self. I trawled them all, one after the one, realising how utterly clueless I was. Even though Ben was just your average sixteen-year-old boy, he had clearly been leading me up the garden path. He'd had an agenda from the start. On re-reading the emails, I could sense how desperate I was for attention, how naive I was, how much I thought that being sexually attractive to someone was the main indicator of 'success'. Something to report back on to the other girls at school. Those emails are a script for a horror movie, but my older self could see exactly what had happened, in clear black and white. Yes, I was clueless – but I was not to blame. There's nothing *wrong* with the content of any of my emails or texts, it was just the fact that they of course were not supposed to be shared. The whole point was I was taking a risk, experimenting, trying stuff out, and wanted it all to remain private.

The thing about being shamed online at such a young age is that you learn your lesson rather quickly, and from then on I thought differently about what I shared with who, which may have been a blessing in disguise. Luckily for me, Ben clearly had *some* sort of conscience and he deleted the forum once I found out about it. Ben was the type of boy who still had Mummy make his packed lunches for school and cut off the crusts, so there was no way he was going to want to get in any sort of trouble for shady Internet action. Whether the actual page got deleted or not didn't matter that much to me, though; the emotional damage was done and it took me a while to really trust anyone again on the Internet.

But the good thing about being a younger teenager is you do bounce back. I wouldn't ever wish any bullying on anyone, but being the victim of a few horrible incidents I can honestly say it prepared me for the inevitable dickheads I'd meet later on in life. There's a thickness of the skin that only ever develops with a bit of teenage bullying. If you have ever found yourself in a position where a group of giggling girls put heavy rocks in your backpack on a school trip and follow behind you as you struggle to walk up the hill, you're actually in the game for teaching yourself to Shake It Off. It was good for me. The bullies, however, suffered later on in life with delayed guilt.

Since the incident with Ben, I have definitely been more careful about what I post online, or text to other people, and in general what I decide to put out there. There's that five-second pause before I hit 'post', and even with my blog I will wait overnight and sleep on it to make sure I mean what I say. But a young girl being sexually shamed by a sixteen-year-old boy opens up a wider conversation, one that isn't just about posting an opinionated blog post.

Women and girls sharing their stories or nude photos or sexual content isn't the issue. It's the Internet Shamers who have the problem. The ones who take it upon themselves to share images or information that wasn't theirs to share. It would be hard to ignore the fact that I felt Ben had the power over me in this situation because he was a guy and I was a girl. The whole thing reeked of double standards. The boys grouped together to point out how awful and hilarious it all was, but Ben was never shamed for expressing *his* sexual feelings. I suppose it was one of my earliest run-ins with sexism, the fact that boys could say whatever they wanted, or share all sorts of sexual content, but I was a girl who was meant to 'behave' and not say anything too sexual. In short, I wasn't entitled to the same freedom of expression. Ben should have kept our conversations private, but I wasn't wrong to have texted him in that way. I was a hormonal teenager wanting to have an outlet for self-experimentation.

People posting things online without consent, like the ex-partners of celebrities who post sex tapes that we unfortunately read about in the news, is a constant online problem and most often it's women who are on the receiving end. We see it happening now with revenge porn: men or women who shame their ex-partners online with nude pictures or tapes in order to make them feel their most vulnerable or to mess up their professional credibility. There are stories of men holding their ex-girlfriends to ransom, charging them money in exchange for not posting the nude photos. Then there was the 4chan leak of female celebrity nudes, pictures that were taken in the security of the women's homes and stolen and republished. Sometimes, it's just a threat, such as with the 4chan countdown threatening to release nude photos of Emma Watson right after she delivered her incredible feminist HeForShe speech at the United Nations headquarters (no images were ever released). These were the same culprits who leaked the nude photos of Jennifer Lawrence. She refused to be shamed, and spoke eloquently to *Vanity Fair* about how the fault lies not with women expressing sexual feelings – often meant for loving partners – but

43

the perpetrators: 'It's my body, and it should be my choice, and the fact that it is not my choice is absolutely disgusting. I can't believe that we even live in that kind of world.'

It's not okay to publish private material when that person doesn't want you to publish it. Even without taking into account the sexism that often underlies this behaviour, it's also just common decency. Where's the Internet police when you need them?

As I've mentioned, since my own early experience I have always been more careful sharing private, personal information with people I've only just met online. This is why youngsters love Periscope, Snapchat and Vine – it's tricky to screenshot something that only lasts seconds and makes the experience of sharing feel safer. But, equally, you can't live your life hoping that someone won't print out that bitchy email you wrote to your colleague. Everything you do *could* be printed and put in a public forum. It's worth being aware of in a world of 'hacks' and 'leaks'. But what can you do? Refuse to go back on the Internet? Never write anything about yourself? Never get naked or enjoy sexy texts? Never tell the truth?

Life is about living and if that means taking a few risks, then so be it. People who break trust and social boundaries are the ones to blame and re-educate. I will continue to overshare. If anyone's going to put weird shit on the Internet about me, it's going to be me who does it.

'The idea of finding your soul mate, whether it's online or not, is what people want.'

Nev Schulman, host of MTV's hit series Catfish

chapter 3
The Day My Friend Got an Internet Boyfriend

2003

We were labelled the Oddballs. We were the ones who didn't fit into the other tribes at school. We weren't the geeks, the horse-riders or the Brunettes (a group of very good-looking brown-haired, brown-eyed girls, types of girls that go on #girliehols and hashtag things like #gorgeousgirls #gorgeouscity). We weren't like the Blondes, either (a group of very good-looking blonde-haired, blue-eyed girls who spent 80 per cent of school time braiding each other's hair like ponies). Nor were we the Goths, the musical geniuses, the Mean Girls or the sporty ones. We were just us. The ones that couldn't, and didn't want to, fit into any sort of category.

We were all different shapes and sizes, and varying person-alities. We each had our own commitments to our interests and went to different after-school clubs, making us independent of each other. I had drama club, the others had piano lessons or charity work or were writing a sci-fi book based on the computer game Theme Hospital. You could say that the one thing we all had in common was that we didn't have anything in common. Our differences ironically brought us all together, like the cast of *Toy Story*, and we became best of friends. We took an interest in each other's unique hobbies and weird habits, and genuinely understood whenever anyone had the recurring problem of feeling like an outsider. We would egg each other on to be our truest, weirdest selves. We kept a group diary and Sellotaped a tampon (a clean one, don't worry, we weren't monsters) inside it to use as the diary bookmark. We'd get into trouble, too, whether it was for smoking roll-ups behind the sports hall using a page of the Bible as a Rizla (we'd seen someone do it in a film), or for trying to make a girl in the class levitate through witchcraft. This never seemed to work, strangely – we'd just repeat 'light as a feather, stiff as a board' until one of us got bored and wandered off.

My friend Gwen and I would talk on the phone for hours (and I mean hours) after school. Our parents were baffled at what we could *possibly have left to talk about* after having been joined at the hip and chatting all day for eight hours at school. I cannot imagine being able to keep a conversation going for that long now. Mainly, we'd list the many reasons why we believed we would never have a boyfriend and have conference calls in which we'd brainstorm how we'd go about catching one, like we were fishermen discussing our hooks and baits. We'd both had a few (gross) snogs and other awkward fumblings (including my online episode with Ben), or texted guys on and off, and we'd even both kissed the same boy right after each other at a party, but we always felt that we would never be one of those girls who had a long-term, loving boyfriend. They were other-worldly beings. We were far from 'safe' girlfriend material.

Day after day, after we got home from school, we would lie upside-down on our beds, hair hanging down over the edge, and discuss how we could better ourselves. At this point in our sad teenage lives, being attractive to the opposite sex was the only thing that mattered, and it was the only thing we didn't feel we could ever be. This perfect boyfriend would, in our dream scenario, have all these qualities:

1. Be nice, but not creepy nice.

2. Wear a non-cringe pair of shoes (very important).

3. Have mates who weren't 'lads', i.e. wouldn't tie you to a tree and pour beer on your head for a 'laugh'.

4. Make us snort-laugh at least seven times a day.

5. Never puke when drunk, ever.

6. Be good-looking, but not good-looking enough for us to think he might get stolen away.

7. Be well-behaved enough for our parents to really like him.

8. Have a good solid haircut and a neck that wasn't the same thickness as his head.

9. Write us poetry, although this wasn't compulsory.

10. Call and text us all the time, mainly so Gwen and I wouldn't have to call each other so much.

That was it; we didn't think our list was unrealistic. We just wanted a really nice guy, who would wear a good-quality jumper and who was called Tom, or something. Really, we just wanted someone safe and inoffensive. Someone who could accompany us to parties and who had a nice smile in photos. It wasn't much to ask.

We wouldn't be pining all the time, of course: we would spend our evenings putting on plays, dressing up in ballgowns, singing into hairbrushes while pretending we were Nelly Furtado and experimenting with make-up in the most absurd ways. Gwen wore brightly coloured corduroy flares and covered her bedroom in photos and sketch drawings from high-end fashion shoots. We were kindred spirits, united in our strangeness, and sometimes our train-track braces really hurt our mouths at the same time – the ultimate teenage bond.

One morning at school, as we waited for our form tutor to come in and take the register, Gwen sidled in next to me with a massive grin across her face.

Pausing for what seemed like an eternity, she smiled and glanced at the floor.

'I've met someone,' she whispered.

'Met SOMEONE? OMG, tell me everything!' I was trying to mask my obvious jealousy.

'Yeah. He's called Marcus. He's a guy from Exeter School. He's … lovely.'

'Where did you meet? How did you meet?' I asked, leaning in closely.

I tried to remain calm and not seem at all desperate to figure out how on earth this had happened so quickly without me being involved (and whether this Marcus dude had any eligible friends. But I'd have to wait a little longer before going in with that question).

'Sounds stupid but we met online. MSN. But I dunno …' she said, flicking her hair behind her shoulder.

'Sounds GREAT!' I could see how happy she was. It was instant. Someone taking an interest could make such a difference to her outlook on herself, on her whole life, it seemed. But as Gwen was my main person to chat to whenever I was feeling insecure about my own attractiveness, I had to try to suppress my feelings of jealousy. I was happy for my friend, but I was so envious, too. Who would I call in my miserable, lonely moments? Was I going to be the only one in the world without anyone taking an interest in me?

Our other friend Angelica overheard the conversation. In fact, she was sitting next to us pretending to read a copy of *Mizz* magazine the whole time. She was one of those girls at school who seemed to have no close friends, despite being sociable – almost over-sociable – with everyone. She would float around on her own, joining and un-joining conversations, flitting in and out of whatever group she fancied at the time. She would meddle. Eager to join this particular conversation, she claimed to know Marcus really well, as they used to go to primary school together.

'You guys talking about Marcus Richards? Our families are friends! He's turned into a right fox. Go G!' Angelica was always so *chirpy*.

She reminded me of a meerkat. It was the way she moved but also her facial features, which were incredibly small and pointy. All the guys that attended the all-boys' school across the road were obsessed with her for being 'cute'. This sort of response from the boys meant she would also enjoy acting like the baby in any social situation, which made people want to carry her bag for her or even put *her* in their bag like a tiny dog. She seemed coy and sweet, but there was undeniably something more complicated beneath the surface. She would teach us 'tricks' to get boys to fancy us, like pretending to type drunk on MSN. 'Try it, they think it's cute,' she would say, twizzling a piece of hair.

'Gwen! *Amazing!* Is he your boyfriend?' Angelica flung her arms around Gwen with no warning, pinning her hands down by her sides.

'Um, no! I don't know! We've only just started chatting. He added me on MSN like two nights ago. Out of the blue.' Gwen was turning a hot pink colour, but the teacher walked in before we could talk any more.

Soon enough, 10 a.m. came around and the bell went, calling break time.

'Why don't you ask him to be your boyfriend tonight?' Angelica whispered.

'Ange, that is the worst advice ever. I'll be laughed at.'

There was something about Angelica that made me really protective of any of my friends who came into contact with her. While she was always at pains to be 'really nice', I suspected that underneath she was rather cunning, trying, somehow, to manipulate others. Even from a young age I was always wary of super-nice people. I just didn't trust them – still don't. No one is ever super, super-nice all the time. If they are, they are probably offloading their darker thoughts behind your back, or they own a voodoo doll. That's why it was important for me and my friends to have our catty arguments if we needed to, fighting it out like siblings. I felt much more comfortable with someone lashing out in the heat of the moment and then apologising later on. At least it meant someone was brave enough to tell the truth.

That evening, Gwen and I had a tennis lesson at our local sports centre. We were both in the same group (although she had always been way better at all sports than me) so we travelled there together on the 57 bus. I loved this bus journey, as it was our regular slot in the week to have proper one-on-one chats. Teenage friendships, looking back, were always far more intense than in adult life. We spent so much time together; we'd sleep in the same bed, cry on each other's laps, and tell each other our deepest, weirdest feelings. I felt properly *in love* with my friends. My friendships nowadays are not as suffocatingly close, but those teenage bonds never properly wear off. They are always there, holding you together like invisible pieces of string. There was a time when Gwen stayed at my house for five days in a row and took a pair of knickers from my under-wear drawer as and when without having to ask.

'When are you going to meet up with Marcus then?' I asked, in between bites of my sausage roll. I was always eating something that defeated the object of actually doing exercise.

'I don't know – we haven't discussed that yet. He hasn't men-tioned it.'

'Are you nervous?'

'A bit, yeah.'

'Don't be.'

'But … look at me.'

'Stop it. You're great. But hey, we could try out some new make-up and outfits later at your house, just in case he asks?'

We'd only just discovered doing eyeliner flicks earlier that week and couldn't help but feel that adding some definition to our eyes was kind of life-changing.

Later, we were at Gwen's house on her massive family computer in the smallest room, practically sitting on each other's laps. It was a huge white clunky machine that looked like it belonged in a museum. The keyboard was incredibly heavy and each button was quite hard to press down. It was practically a typewriter, with a dial-up connection that sounded like aliens were about to land. We logged in and heard the familiar sound of someone coming online at the same time. It was Marcus.

Gwen's eyes lit up and she clicked back her fingers, ready to type.

Marcus: Hey sexy

Gwen: Hey

M: How are you 2day

G: GOOD THANKS WOOPS!!!! CAP LOCKS!

M: How was tennis

G: Really fun – thanks – we played well i think!

G: Marcus can I see another picture of you . :) Your MSN one is a bit blurry and small.

M: Sure! Although you will see me when we meet :)

G: I know, but it'd be nice to visualise who I'm talking to!

M: Of course. UMMMMM just finding one on my computer now ;)

G: YAY

M: ...

Their conversation was slightly stunted, and Marcus suddenly went offline. To me, there was something a bit fishy about all this, but I didn't say anything because I knew how happy it was making her. We pretended it was no big deal and went downstairs to watch TV. It was probably fine. At worst, it was probably just some creep from Exeter School who wanted to get in her pants. From watching their snippet of conversation I could see they didn't really *talk* much, but hey, who was I to judge after my own mortifying attempts at Internet flirting with Ben. Each to their own. I wasn't exactly an expert in that department.

It was the school holidays and Angelica and her family went on holiday for a week. This meant there could be no meddling in the Marcus situation, which was a relief. However, Gwen was upset because Marcus had only logged on twice in the week and spoken to her for about five minutes each time. She was worried he'd gone off her. She suffered with anxiety from a young age and her fingers would twitch and her heart would start beating out of her chest. It often took the whole group of us to calm her down and stop her shaking.

So when Angelica returned from her holidays, Gwen couldn't help but ask her if she knew what was up with Marcus going AWOL, in case she had any intel on the situation, given he was a family friend. Angelica had no idea, but she invited us around for dinner after school so we could discuss it in detail, because she loved a gossip. We said yes, mainly because her mum was a really good cook and made a banging lasagne. Our stomachs would lead the way in most situations.

Later that night I asked Angelica if I could use her computer to quickly see if the boy I fancied was online (as much as I was invested in the Marcus situation, I had my own fish to fry). I went onto hotmail.com (as you did back then), and weirdly, it automatically loaded up marcus192190@hotmail.com's inbox. Suddenly all of Marcus's emails were staring back at me, as in *Gwen's* Marcus. How? I mean, he must have come round to her house and left himself logged in. I felt so guilty to have stumbled across his private emails but I couldn't help looking more closely, as it was all so odd. The majority of the emails in his inbox were confirmation emails signing up to fashion newsletter websites. In addition, there was a confirmation that he'd set up his MSN account only a few weeks ago. There was nothing in this inbox that gave a clue to Marcus's personality, or what he was into, or any emails among friends or family. It was spooky and empty. None of it made sense, at all. He didn't seem very interesting. I couldn't see any real traces of personality.

I kept quiet about what I'd found and went back to Gwen's to stay the night. She dumped her bag and immediately ran up the stairs to see if Marcus was online. He'd just gone offline. Angelica, on the hand, just logged on, making that oh-so-familiar MSN sign-in noise.

'Hi girlies!!!' she typed.

She used the 'nudge' button a few times.

We had gone to make a up of tea in the kitchen, loudly discussing a spooky text message I'd received from an unknown number.

As we went back into the 'computer room', Marcus's user name popped up, and Angelica had gone.

I sat next to her playing Snake on my phone, waiting for Gwen to give me an update on her digital love life.

'Oh my God,' Gwen said in a low tone.

'Hmm?' I looked up. 'Come here. This is so weird. He has just said hello to me but his font is Comic Sans and it's PINK. Do you think he's been hacked?'

There was one thing I knew from being an avid MSN user, and that was the fact that everyone has a different font and colour. It was like having your own signature perfume. I knew that pink Comic Sans, in bold, was Angelica's font. I was blue Trebuchet, Gwen's was purple italic Lucia Handwriting. The boy I fancied, Tim, was black bold Times New Roman (clearly a very sensible type). Marcus was dark blue Arial. I couldn't understand why Marcus was suddenly typing in the same font as Angelica. It was bizarre. Angelica had just been online. Either they were together at Angelica's house using the same computer, or ...

My brain was ticking.

Either way, Angelica or Marcus had forgotten to change the font back to his Arial font in dark blue before chatting to Gwen.

'G, something weird's going on here. Don't be freaked out. But I think Angelica has been logging into Marcus's account and sending you emails from it.'

'Huh?'

'I went onto her computer at her house earlier, and when I went onto Hotmail, Marcus's inbox was open,' I explained.

Gwen's eyes were darting all over the place.

'The weird thing is that he had hardly any emails, it was all just subscription emails, so it must have been a newly created account ...' I wrapped my fingers around my chin, like I was trying to solve a murder mystery.

Gwen looked hurt. 'That's so odd. So … do you think …?'

We were both thinking the same thing.

We looked at each other in silence. Maybe Angelica wasn't hacking into Marcus's account. *Maybe Angelica was Marcus.* It would explain a lot, including the fact that Marcus hardly went online during the week that Angelica went on her family holiday. It would explain the fact that Marcus confusingly had the same Comic Sans font as Angelica. It would explain how Angelica was 'accidentally' signed in to Marcus's Hotmail, knew his password and had the same date of birth. It would explain the fact that Angelica knew so much about this guy who no one else had ever heard of. We were going to confront her tomorrow: had she made up this boy? And why? Why would she have done that?

The next day at school was as awkward as we had predicted. Angelica was sitting on her desk, reading from her geography textbook with her big hazel eyes fluttering, looking as innocent as a character out of *Bambi*. We felt like lions creeping up on a deer sipping from the watering hole.

'Hey guys! How was your sleepover?' Angelica spotted us and her bright wide eyes looked genuinely interested in how we both were.

'Umm. Yeah, we're fine. Look Angelica, we've got something to say to you. Well, something to ask you.' I breathed in. Gwen stood a little behind me, clearly absolutely dreading the conversation that was about to take place. Angelica looked confused. I continued.

'We need to talk about Marcus.'

'Oh no! Is he okay?' She looked at her shoes.

'We know it's you.' Having said it out loud, I suddenly felt guilty and hot in the face.

'W–w–what do you mean?' Angelica shuffled back on the desk, like a frightened pet. Before we could say anything else, she picked up her books and vanished. I felt bad for questioning her in front of the whole classroom. She'd managed to worm her way out of it, and I didn't blame her.

Later on, I found Angelica in the music room, the highest room in the tallest building on our school campus. She was early for our music lesson and I thought it would be a good time to confront her, privately. I was genuinely interested in finding out the truth, but thought I'd do it without the others watching. I felt protective over Gwen and couldn't help myself. Plus I was intrigued.

I sat down beside her on one of the old wooden chairs for a few minutes.

'Did you make him up?' I asked, softly.

Angelica looked like she was about to cry. She bowed her head.

'Look. I know this sounds ridiculous … I know you will think this is stupid,' she began, 'but … I just … I felt sorry for Gwen. I was just going to do it for a week to make her smile and then I got carried away. I just wanted her to be happy. I wanted her to know that someone could like her. That she is capable of being liked. She's a really good friend. Now I don't know what to do.' Angelica's head was in her hands, and she was shaking. I put my hand on the back of her shoulder, telling her not to worry.

I recently reminded Gwen of this strange episode, in the pub one Sunday in east London where we both live. She shrugged, as she took a drag from her cigarette in a Jessa-from-*Girls* kind of way. 'I mean, it was quite sweet, really,' she said.

The thing is, Angelica wasn't a malicious person. She still isn't. She did something a bit silly, but I probably did worse things to my friends back then. I faked all sorts of things. I still fake things now. Gwen and I laugh about it still because it is a bizarre example of how you can be deceived by the people you least expect through the Internet. We realised how easy it was to pull off, but also how easy it was to find out the truth. We were so young. Nowadays we are probably a lot better at covering our tracks, knowing more about the technology that we use. People con us every day, and anyone can make up a fake online identity, remaining completely anonymous. In our early teens, we'd had an education in how easy it could be to pretend to be other people. From then on we were constantly on the lookout so, in the long term, it was probably a positive experience. Not to mention quite innocent. It had started out as a nice thing to do for a friend that had just got a bit out of hand.

The word 'catfish' seems to be now part of our everyday lingo. In 2010, a documentary film called *Catfish*, directed by Nev Schulman, was released. It was a film all about how the person he'd fallen in love with on Facebook didn't turn out to be that person at all. Instead of a young woman named Megan, Nev found himself meeting a forty-year-old married woman called Angela. Angela, lonely at home, had fabricated an online identity and got so addicted to Nev's attention that she couldn't bring herself to give it up – even when he visited her in person to investigate. After the documentary aired, thousands of people wrote letters of support and advice for Nev, telling him they'd been in similar situations. The reaction to this documentary proved that, all around the world, people were 'dating' or befriending people online who weren't who they said they were.

MTV's *Catfish* (the TV show that came off the back of the documentary) is generally quite dark, and often genuinely upsetting, with real issues at the heart of each story: deep self-esteem problems, jealousy, pathological lying or even sociopathic behaviour. And these deceptions are able to fool us on a bigger and bigger scale. (Although my favourite line out of a *Catfish* episode to date is: 'Do you *really* think he works with Kanye West?' 'Nuff said.)

Think of Belle Gibson, who claimed online that she had cured several tumours through healthy eating and alternative therapies alone, and who became a 'role model' to thousands of young girls and cancer sufferers. She got as far as selling her book to a publisher before the truth was uncovered and we learned that there were serious health-related elements of her story that were made up. Journalists have tried in vain to get to the bottom of her story, but the deceptions are so difficult to untangle that it's almost impossible to see who the 'real' Belle might be.

Angelica's story is, of course, less extreme, and I don't think she got a buzz from simulating another person, but she did start off with a small idea and it escalated quickly. A story like this includes just a few white lies, designed to make a friend feel more loved, but ends up becoming something bigger and more complicated. It's very easy to see how tempting it could be to want to become someone else for a short period of time.

In fact, in some ways you could argue that people pretend to be different versions of themselves online every day. Having a social profile means you can make your life look way better than it is. Aren't we all guilty of this to some degree? Does your profile picture really look like you? Did you *really* have the 'best day ever'? Are you catfishing someone if you edit pictures of your food to within an inch of your life and don't admit that in fact the restaurant you're in is not all that special? Are you catfishing someone if you edit spots out of your selfies? Or if you upload a picture of a picnic hamper in the park pretending to still be there in the sunshine when really you're on your sofa under a blanket eating Domino's pizza?

Once you make something up, it's hard to stop for lots of different reasons. Having had this experience happen to my friend so early on, I felt lucky to be knowledgeable about how people could potentially fake it online and how to find them out. I knew that I'd have to be savvy and suss people out online before meeting up to make sure I was getting an honest representation of them. Angelica's catfishing episode had made me more switched on. After all, I had been the one who had spotted that something wasn't quite right. Hopefully, I thought to myself, I would never be conned by someone online.

You can probably guess that I was. But before then, there were other, even murkier Internet dangers to overcome.

'just spooning my boyfriend
out of his container
my boyfriend is ice cream'

@StarbucksQu33n

chapter 4

Google Ruins My First IRL
Relationship

2005

'Be yourself!' the teenage magazines chanted at me, each page displaying a toned, tanned model laughing while wearing silk pyjamas and eating a bio yoghurt. This same slogan would also be sold on little T-shirts in Etam clothing stores and hung off cheap necklaces. It was everywhere I went. *Be yourself.*

The problem was, I had no idea who I was. And if I did, I was petrified of letting her out. I felt like a trapped Miley Cyrus before she was brave enough to whip off her Hannah Montana wig. The more I could hide behind mass popular culture, friends' opinions or things that had been 'okayed' by my friendship group the better. I would have acceptable vanilla thoughts in public and scribble all my true feelings in my silver diary, sticking in ripped-out pages from TV guides, analysing song lyrics and pictures of young couples snogging. I would hide away all of the music, CDs, films and books I liked, because no one else had mentioned they had liked them too. In my teen brain this meant only one thing: that I was a loser with weird taste. Playing Meat Loaf and Cher's 'Dead Ringer For Love' definitely would not go down well with the friends who only had eyes for B*Witched. I was still reading Roald Dahl books but I assumed they were too childish and that I should have grown out of them by then, and it was probably weird that I was still re-reading my favourite parts of *Matilda* every night, or collecting pig ornaments. I found it was easier to hide my true interests and just lay low; it's easier, as a teen, to just nod along with everyone else and keep all your favourite stuff to yourself. I'd Sellotape all my secret loves to my bedroom walls and shout 'Stay out of my room!' to anyone who creaked past my door. Why risk showing people the real you if there is a chance you could get rejected and break into a million pieces? It's always safer to remain mainstream.

I hated the thought of being different. I hated my lightbulb luminous hair, because people would comment on it. Anything that 'stood out' I immediately loathed. I wished that I were thinner; that my mum would let me wear school shoes with a heel; that I didn't have freckles. It's sad to look back on how cripplingly insecure you are as a teenager, questioning every strand of your personality, moulding things into shape in order to 'fit in'. I don't know a single teenager who liked themselves during school. Every ounce of my energy went into attempting to fit in or just to flat out avoid being noticed.

Now, as I sit here at the age of twenty-six, everything I do is pretty much about *not* fitting in. I argue with other people's opinions, I want to be noticed, I don't like nightclubs or wearing plain clothes or doing the same things as other people 'just because'. I like dyeing my hair random colours, writing things on my blog that raise eyebrows, experimenting with bright vintage clothes and attempting to discover things first. Of course, this is hardly *rebellion*. This is still just a middle-class middle finger to society. But the point is, I'm not overly into just being a sheep like I was as a teen. Being a teenager was about being a member of a very boring herd, often being led by someone who would one day be totally irrelevant to you; someone who if you spotted them on public transport now, you would avoid by hiding behind a newspaper.

I was on a journey, like all other girls and boys my age, to discover who I was, and who I was happy being. Our lives are made up of lots of different people, places and events. We are just walking human stories. Whatever happens, we come out of the other side learning a lot about ourselves. There was no way I was going to learn to 'be myself' without some mistakes along the way.

In 2005 I was sixteen, chubby with wonky train-track braces on my teeth. It was just another evening after school. I'd eaten quickly and rushed to the computer room, logging on to desperately flirt online with a boy called Max. He was a couple of years older than me. At this stage in my Internet life, I liked to think I was quite witty online. I'd been practising. I was a fast typist with a good tone, and I'd been saving up some good jokes and had some interesting anecdotes up my sleeve (none of them mine). I was a teenage introvert posing as an extrovert, spouting sarcasm, winky emoticons and bold statements while sitting totally silently in my pyjamas in my parents' house. I'd write 'LOL' but I wouldn't laugh. The words came out of my fingertips, and I came across as full of energy on screen even when I felt deflated in the flesh. I would distil all my brain power into the keyboard and feel strangely powerful. I had an intuition that a lot of good things were going to come from my new-found confidence from behind a screen. Things were a bit shit in real life, but online, I felt like this was my *in*.

Max was an unconventional crush, in the sense that my friends didn't 'get it'. But he had totally captured my teenage imagination; I had real feelings for him that of course were later laughable, but at the time were really quite overwhelming. He was the big brother of a girl in my school year called Laura, which instantly made him appear 100 per cent cooler than me simply by virtue of being older and the fact he was off limits. Laura would have been grossed out if she knew. I was up for the challenge to woo him over the Internet, even if MSN was the only medium available. Even at fifteen I was quite cunning. I would go round to Laura's house most Wednesdays – I found out through a series of casual questions that this was the only day Max didn't have some sort of after-school sporting activity – and we'd all get the bus to their house together. During the journey, I would try to sound sophisticated and intelligent when talking to Laura, as I changed from my school uniform into my best clothes (purple rollneck jumpers and cord flares at this age), even though Max always had headphones in and couldn't have cared less. Laura was none the wiser to my secret agenda, though we were becoming best friends. I would make sure to 'accidentally' bump into Max around the house. He was so much taller and broader than all the boys my age. It was a case of this: I didn't want Aaron Carter. I wanted Nick Carter. It was *all* about the older brother.

I'd been to Laura's place a few times for parties (they had a pool), and Max would often hide away in his room, coming out every so often to get something from the fridge in his low-slung jogging bottoms (I think he'd been watching a lot of American TV). I'd do that classic (awful) flirting technique of coincidentally needing something from the fridge at the same time as him, reacting like a meerkat on heat every time I heard him make his way down the stairs. I'd make slight conversation ('The fridge door is a bit creaky, isn't it?') and then I'd go back to the kids' table frowning at my lame attempt to make conversation. Max would be completely oblivious and go back upstairs with his protein shake under his arm, downing orange juice from the carton, off to do something a bit cooler. Or just to have a wank, probably.

It was one random summer's evening that I first noticed that Max had added me on MSN. I was surprised, considering the last time I saw him I was playing Twister with Laura and had split my trousers while making a very ambitious 'right-hand yellow'. I realised that, yes, he was slightly socially inept in real life, with his stunted conversation and his refusal to make eye contact, but still I wanted to give it a go. Maybe he was more fun if you just got to know him, I thought – and to my surprise his true colours did come out on MSN. Online he was hilarious, demonstrating a flair for witty one-liners, and we'd often get talking about loads of deep and meaningful 'life stuff'. What we wanted to *be*, stuff that made us sad, the things that frustrated us at school, what we dreamed about and what we worried about at night. When you're online past your bedtime, talking to your friend's older brother, it really does feel quite exciting when you're sixteen.

I told a few friends and they were secretly quite impressed. Having approval from my group of mates meant everything to me, especially when it came to boys, even though the air was thick with competition and tension at this age. The passive-aggressive comments would start to roll in: 'Are you sure he likes you in *that way* though, Em?', 'I don't want you to get hurt', or 'I wouldn't get too into it, he's had some really gorgeous girlfriends in the past.' I could see what they meant. He wasn't exactly the type of guy to propose to me on a beach wearing white linen trousers. He was a rugby player who was into rap music and obsessed with the gym. I noticed, on sneaking past his bedroom one night when I was having a sleepover with Laura, that Max's screensaver on his Windows computer was a picture of himself, flexing his own bicep. This, more than anything, should have been a warning sign.

His MSN status would normally consist of deep song lyrics and I soon realised that I could bond with him by Googling the song lyric he'd quoted and reeling off some weird facts about the band, or pretending to love the song too. He was obviously surprised, as the songs were clearly so niche and most likely illegally downloaded from LimeWire. It was normally some B-side from a nineties rap band that I'd never heard of. But I clued myself up using online music forums and I could tell he was impressed. This soon started to become an obsession, faking my interests to grab his attention and affection. I realised that I could become an expert in pretty much anything if I had a spare thirty minutes. *How brilliant. I would never have awkward small talk again, thanks to Google!* This was my road to realising that I could learn about new stuff very quickly and never not know what anyone was talking about. It helped me pass exams and seem more intelligent in conversations but, dangerously, I could also begin to very easily fake things – and by things, I mean myself: my own personality.

Every evening was the same. I'd log in (after 6 p.m. – it was cheaper) and wait for thirty-five minutes; I could see that Max was online, but I was too scared to talk to him first. I'd go and grab some snacks from the kitchen, then I would sit and wait, changing my status to 'offline' then 'online' again at least five times so that my little MSN would pop up and make a *'dun-dun!'* sound, in case he'd missed seeing me log in the first time. Later in life I realised they never do 'miss seeing you the first time'. They saw you. They were ignoring you. (The same logic also applies to work emails.)

Here are the rules for online crushes that I did not follow, for quite some years:

1. Do not text twice.

2. Do not keep deleting and re-adding the object of your affection on MSN.

3. Do not log in multiple times. (Everyone knows what you're trying to do.)

4. Don't create another account with a different name and creep around.

5. Don't ask him immediately about ex-girlfriends.

6. Don't text him and then follow up with 'WHOOPS WRONG NUMBER!'

7. Don't change your status to something cryptic about him.

8. Don't pretend to be your friend and ask if he likes you.

9. Don't pretend to dramatically hate him.

10. Don't pretend 'something awful has happened' to make him talk to you.

11. Don't pretend to fancy his mate.

12. Don't cry at him.

If only I knew the Twelve Internet Commandments back then. If only.

After waiting for what seemed like an eternity, I realised that, if I wanted to talk to Max, I'd have to pipe up first. After all, by now I should have realised that it was only once in a blue moon that I'd get the 'hi wuu2' said to me first. It was like a game. It's nice to be spoken to first, and it's what society tells you should happen: the boys *ask*, the girls reply. But it seems that boys don't really tend to overthink these things too much. Sometimes they make the first move, sometimes they don't. No explanation needed. No scientific analysis needed to be carried out. If only I knew back then that not every tiny sentence needed to be ripped apart and inspected like a poor frog in an A-level biology class. I did not need to get my friends round with notepads and pretend we were in a workshop to analyse a text with three words in it.

Over time, I realised I was morphing and changing my personality, aligning things to fit in with his interests, like an optical illusion. Every time he mentioned a band he liked, I'd Google all the albums or the lyrics, and reel off this supreme 'knowledge' as though I was also a massive fan. Same with the TV he watched, or his sports interests, or the last place he'd been on holiday. I was addicted to matching my 'personality' with his, like a fun little jigsaw puzzle. Every time we got talking in our little online world, I wasn't showing any fragment of the real me. I didn't even know who the real me was. It was a game, making sure that his response was always: 'Woahhhh, this is sick. I didn't know we had so much in common!'

I'd wait for his surprised reaction and give myself a little high five. Little did I know that it was okay to not have *everything* in common with one's crush. In real life, it's too spooky and doesn't give you anything to debate or playfully fight over. In reality you don't want to go out with a twin version of yourself who just nods along to everything you say. I was like a creepy portable mirror that kept following him around. I was surprised that my weird strategy *seemed* to be actually working. I clearly had never heard the phrase 'opposites attract' before. In hindsight, I must have been extremely annoying. But at the time, I thought I was being so cunning, knowing how to use the Internet to pretend to be someone's 'other half'. After my trickery, he must *surely* be in love with me. He would never have this insane bond with any other girl, *ever*, because it would be impossible – mainly because they weren't using my genius Google-dependent plan.

Max was really into *Dr Who*. I knew the day of the week it was on but I never watched it and I had no interest in ever watching it. I would just Google plot lines and character names and go along with the conversation. I'd look at what music he was playing (on MSN you could stream your 'now playing' list so all your friends could see) and I would change mine to a song by the same artist, or to another track on the same album. *Cunning.*

So it didn't take long until Max asked me round to his house. I knew this must be because he'd realised we were a 'match'. He said he'd come and pick me up in his car (yes! A boy who could drive!). I was running late from a shopping session with my mum, mainly spent in WHSmith looking for new stationery for school (cool), and we raced home just in time for me to go to the loo. A few minutes later, I heard Max pull into the drive in his red Vauxhall Corsa. My phone buzzed.

'I'm in your drive :)'

My stomach tightened with nerves and I hopped out of the door, shouting up the stairs to my mum that I'd be home later on tonight. After all, this was just going to be an innocent date. We'd probably just watch TV together. I'd be home that same evening. As we drove down the Exeter roads, in and out of country lanes, we arrived at Max's house, a beautiful bungalow in a tiny, pictur-esque village.

'My parents aren't in, by the way,' he said casually.

I peered into Laura's room as we walked down the corridor and was relieved to see she wasn't in either. I really didn't want this situation to be any weirder than having Laura hear us flirting through the bedroom walls, as she probably would have charged in demanding an explanation. My palms were clammy as it was and I knew he'd try to interrupt us if he was there, and I couldn't bear the thought of losing him as a friend. It all felt very secretive. I hadn't told anyone, not even my close friends, that I was there.

Max ducked his head in a cabinet, producing a bottle of red wine and two glasses.

I wasn't a huge drinker, mainly because I was still underage, but also since finding myself asleep in a flowerbed a few weeks previ-ously after a rogue outing with friends to Exeter's finest (grossest) underage-serving pubs I'd been a bit put off. But this was different, I was on a date with a seventeen-year-old; this was sophisticated. We were sipping (his parents' Merlot), not downing straight vodka shots. I was more grown-up now.

We sat on the edge of his bed in his room, sipping our grown-up wine and watching two episodes of *Dr Who*. I was totally bored off my face. I had spent the last four months pretending to be a total fangirl in order to woo him, pretending I'd been to all the conventions, and I was trying to laugh and comment intelligently in all the right places. It seemed to be working. I even managed to bring up some really geeky *Dr Who* stuff that I had found on the deepest, darkest, strangest online fan forums. He kept digging his elbow into me at a 'really good bit' and mouthing all the words, and I'd have to smile and nod along and look interested. God, even *I* felt I was getting too good at this. *Maybe I could be an actress.* My mind began to wander.

Then the weirdest thing happened. Max turned off the TV, quite abruptly, and put on Microsoft Media Player (these were the days before Spotify). I noticed that he had labelled this particular selection of songs 'The Make-out Playlist'. This was and is completely horrifying for two reasons: 1) 'make-out' is an American word, which a British boy should *not* be using, and 2) that was *very* presumptuous. It was the preparation that had started to baffle me. The perfectly laid-out wine and glasses. The fact that he'd shooed his parents out of the house for a few hours, and now this playlist …

All I remember of this strange playlist was 'Feeling Good' by Muse and 'Hey Mama' by the Black Eyed Peas, which I thought was an odd mix. It wasn't remotely sexy; it just felt weird. Weird that he'd spent time selecting songs for us to kiss to. Maybe it was romantic, in some strange, pre-prepared way. But it was also quite creepy.

A few minutes after letting the playlist run, Max quickly put down his wine glass and leaned in for the kill. His massive arms squeezed around me, pretty much suffocating me and digging into my boobs, but I went along with it. After all, this is what my plan had been leading up to. I wanted this. So I thought.

He kissed my neck, and before I knew it my top and bra were off, with him nuzzling in my boobs. I realised, as he threw it onto the other side of the bed, that I was wearing a really old red bra, with straps that were hanging on by a thread. As my jeans came off – after a few tugs – my black and white polka dot pants were on show. His eyebrows furrowed.

'Oh.'

He paused and looked confused.

'I thought all girls wore matching underwear.' He appeared put off.

I immediately frowned. Something wasn't right about a sentence beginning: '*I thought all girls …*'

I was the Bridget Jones of the underwear world. I wore old pants until they were practically broken. Comfort was my greatest joy and I found lace would rub against me uncomfortably. I was a cotton girl and proud: grey, white, black and, on special occasions, i.e. tonight, it was the polka dots, Marks & Spencer's finest. But I'd pretty much pretended to be Sienna Miller in *Layer Cake* via the Internet, so no wonder he'd got excited. The reality was far, far different. I'd catfished him with Google's trusty help.

We continued our dry humping, snogging and gyrating, and I found myself trying to give him a blowjob. My first ever attempt. It was horrendous. His penis was absolutely mammoth and had a life of its own, flicking every which way like a python that didn't want to be held. It would slip out of my hand, slap backwards onto his stomach and slither away from me whenever I tried to put it in my mouth. After about fifteen minutes of trying to slide my mouth up and down I gave up because, quite frankly, my mouth and jaw were starting to hurt, and after a while I was physically aching, like I'd just been to the dentist. They say you shouldn't bite off more than you can chew, and in hindsight I wish he'd been a lot smaller so I could work out what on earth to do with it. I couldn't believe that he had to carry that around with him all day; it was like a small pet.

Max huffed and puffed. He was obviously turned on – and wanted to get his end away – but I got so freaked out after the aching-jaw episode that I just blurted out, 'I'm not having sex with you!' (This later gave me a complex, which manifested for a few years when any boy who spoke to me or showed me any interest whatsoever was subject to my own presumption: 'Ummm, just to manage expectations here, I don't plan on having sex with you.' It made me sound both celibate and arrogant.)

After trying to get me to give in, and I had shaken him off to tend to my aching jaw, Max then turned on me.

'I guess I'll have to finish myself off, then. I think you should order yourself a taxi.'

I could not believe it. I slowly put my clothes back on – at least, the ones I could find easily – and then I just stared at him, hoping for a logical response to all of this. My broad conclusion: teenage boys were sex-obsessed love-rats. And yet I was still clamouring for attention despite being faced with this proof. I asked him timidly what I should do.

'I don't really care how you get home. Think I just heard my mum come in from work; ask her if you can use our home phone to call a taxi.'

The humiliation! Having to leave Max's room, post-coital (or nearly post-coital) blushing cheeks, my top on backwards and no pants (I couldn't find them in a hurry), to ask his mother how to get home because I'd been turfed out of his bedroom.

As I scooped up my belongings into a heap and went to leave his room, I turned around and screamed:

'WELL, GUESS WHAT – I DON'T EVEN LIKE *DOCTOR WHO*! AND I THINK YOUR MUSIC TASTE IS PROPERLY SHIT!'

Before slamming the door.

It was a harsh but helpful education for me: Max was a total dick, but if you have to lie between your teeth in order to get a guy to like you, you're the fool too.

Once I got over the sheer horror of being asked to leave some-body's house because I wouldn't have sex with them, and rushing out with no knickers on, I managed to reflect on the situation in a different way, and even get some positives out of it (I had to, otherwise I might have died from embarrassment and confusion). At least I had escaped. It could have gone dangerously wrong and I would have regretted that being my dreaded 'first time'.

I also took time away from flirting on MSN with boys who made me feel insecure, and I just threw myself into doing the stuff that I actually enjoyed. As a result, I started to learn to be myself. I went back to basics and began to build my own personality from scratch, going back to the roots of the things I enjoyed deep down. (This is something I've had to do multiple times when feeling lost in adult life.) Before, I had been layering my public persona with everyone else's preferences, like a human game of Tetris, trying to win socially acceptable gold stars. The Max episode had made me realise just how much I was morphing my personality into something I *thought* I should be rather than what I really was. Despite the constant reality of peer pressure, I discovered there's nothing more freeing than saying 'no' or speaking up when you like something different.

I started to realise I didn't actually like most of the stuff I was pretending to like. I thought Green Day were crap. Apple sour shots made me gag. Butterfly clips hurt my head. Heavy metal music sounded like dying cats. It felt *so* good to finally start to be myself, to start exploring the things that actually made me tick. I got really into my own kind of music; going to gigs I liked, wearing band T-shirts that I liked, working out what I actually enjoyed, making collages and finding people who I truly clicked with online. I also started to learn how to defend my beliefs and interests. I was getting to know all of the things that *I* enjoyed, not things I thought I would enjoy just because someone else did. It was odd realising that pretty much every element of my teenage personality was made up of stuff other people liked. It was like doing a huge spring clean and putting my fake personality into a bin bag and taking it to the skip.

This, of course, to my present self, is not exactly rocket science. Naturally it makes sense to pursue the things that make you happy and, in doing so, you will meet people who share common interests with you. *But being a teenager is hard.* Really, really hard. Being yourself takes a lot of confidence because you don't ever feel truly normal. No one does. You have to take the risk of telling people the stuff you like, and then keep your fingers crossed that they a) like it too, and b) respect you for it. We all have quirks, secrets, weird obsessions.

From then on, when chatting to anyone, I was able to put the 'real me' out there. I had no strategy. I wouldn't hide anything away. This was the start of me becoming a keen oversharer. In fact, I often found myself oversharing strange information that no one had necessarily asked for. People would occasionally back away, like a beeping loading truck, hoping I wouldn't keep talking at them. But the weird bits of your personality are actually the things that people remember about you and often the very reason someone ends up falling in love with you, eventually. You're more likely to meet someone right for you by being honest about yourself, rather than getting chucked out of someone's bedroom for pretending to be someone else.

Anyway, I wonder what Max did with my pants. And he still owes me £15 for that sad taxi ride home.

'Man will occasionally stumble over the truth, but most of the time he will pick himself up and continue on.'

Winston Churchill

chapter 5

Down the Rabbit Hole

2008

Sometimes, we see things we don't necessarily want to see when we venture onto the Internet. Like a pixelated Alice in Wonderland I'm often riddled with anxiety when I fall down an Internet hole and see some disturbing and strange things that are the equivalent of a caterpillar smoking a spliff. This might range from hardcore six-second Vines live from war zones – the horrific news looping on repeat – to lighter, socially odd things, such as: 'Dave from primary school has quit his job as a top NASA researcher to become a stand-up comedian.'

We see things every day that makes us rub our eyes and squint and think *what*? She's marrying *him*? She's moving to *Alaska*? Julia is now a *pole-dancing teacher*? I'll log into Twitter and someone will have posted a GIF of a terrifying new horror movie, or someone will be in Hawaii on a sun lounger with their iPad, using the hashtag #LivingTheBloggerLife or #LoveLifeLoveSunsets. Both of these things you don't really want to be spontaneously exposed to when you're home alone and feeling vulnerable. Every time we open the lid of our laptops, we are belting ourselves in for an unknown ride.

We're becoming very good at piecing together information too, plucking little clues and titbits from a series of social networks and mutual friend connections to see what people are doing. We are constantly pulling together puzzle pieces without realising, joining the dots, figuring out missing information, because it's rare that someone will post *everything*. We know that sometimes when people don't post to social media for while, it might mean they are out there in the world legitimately *having fun* instead of live-tweeting *Homes Under the Hammer* from the sofa. We know that people save up holiday snaps and post them months later, forcing us to rattle them: *I know you are not really on holiday goddammit – at least put #TBT* [Throwback Thursday] *on your snaps so we know the truth!*

Everyone is looking at everyone else's feeds to try to work out what the truth is about other people's lives, but mainly worrying about creating their own online identity. We know that we're good at displaying, hinting, *suggesting* what our lives look like while leaving lots of puzzle pieces out of frame. The dodgy-looking bits: the arguments, the spaghetti down the T-shirt, the greasy-hair days, doctor's appointments, the super-plus tampons in the trolley, bills, Post Office trips, grocery shopping – all these things are never usually posted. We'd probably never do a post-STI check-up selfie saying, 'I'm all clear, guys!' Social media has never been a natural place for sharing the real stuff. Us human beings have a lot of boring life admin, so we're very good at hiding it online nowadays and only sharing the happy, bright, emoji-filled chunks of our lives, in order to give the illusion we are very happy, well-put-together, mentally stable individuals.

You'd think that seeing other people's happy moments would make us happy, but that's not really how we're wired. Writer Chelsea Fagan launched a website called TheFinancialDiet.com and started a movement called #TotalHonestyTuesday in which she'd share a really honest piece of life news on Instagram instead of a filtered picture of an infinity pool like every other fucker. It could be an unmade bed, a really sad-looking dinner she had made on an off-day or an emotional truth about her relationship with a sibling. A photo of hers would catch me off guard as I scrolled through my Instagram feed, seeing it among the pictures of kale smoothies, tree blossom and inspirational quotes. It felt refreshing to see something so real in front of me. It would make me sit back and reflect for a moment instead of just passively engaging with the rat-race of perfectly filtered photos.

The idea soon caught on, and a group of truth-tellers started posting pictures of their shitty bank balance, or a lying-in-bed-wearing-no-make-up selfie or details of their true down-days. I don't think the Internet should be always about airing our bad days either but, equally, we shouldn't be afraid to post the truth. Chelsea's feed was a mixture of exactly that: aspirational cool-girl stuff vs what it means to be human. It was a brilliant way of show-ing how honest we aren't. My favourite other example is the parody Instagram account @deliciouslystella, which also goes against the grain of 'Instagram perfect'. One picture of 'Stella' (aka comedian Bella Younger) was captioned 'Fab abs!', which was literally some Fab ice-creams strapped to her belly. These accounts are essentially 'breaking the fourth wall' and make us all feel like we can undo a button on our jeans and breathe out.

But even with these forays into honesty there is much that is still staged, and so we are constantly monitoring other people's posts to discover any 'slips' that could tell us something relevant. Even the media hunt down clues online and play Internet detective to try and find out the truth about certain people. A 'news story' can now just consist of Zayn Malik, ex-member of boyband One Direction, 'favouriting' (now changed to 'liking') a selfie taken by Kylie Jenner. *What does this mean?*, the newspapers asked, and impressively managed to dig up at least five different 'angles' on the story.

We take our own angles on what's going on around us too. Who's tweeting who? Who's liking whose stuff? Who's tagged in whose photo? It's like we've morphed into the Perez Hiltons of our own social lives. Sometimes we get it right, but more often than not, we get it very, very wrong. Stalking the girls an ex-boyfriend has started following on Twitter can only spiral into drinking five bottles of wine.

We are all Sherlock Holmes with our magnifying glass, con-stantly inspecting our screens, our friendship circles, strangers, celebrities. We dig up information that is none of our business. Except it's technically all of our business because it's being shown to us daily and, after all, it's public information. We can find out anything we want with a few link-clicks of the mouse and savvy keyword searches. Facebook hoovered up all our information, but it was also the first thing we wanted to give all our informa-tion to. It was new and hard to resist. When they asked us to fill out a profile and started asking us personal questions, we loved it. Hey, any chance to talk about ourselves! It was like we were being interviewed for a magazine, but every day! You want to know my name? My date of birth? The first time I had sex? My mother's maiden name? Oh go on then, you flirt! Please take all of my info! While you're at it, here are my doctor's notes and all of my painful repressed memories! And yes, of course you can go on to sell it to some companies who will then target me at my most emotional and financially vulnerable times. Thanks so much!

With all this glorious information, my newsfeed is now filled with sponsored posts that aim to show me my favourite things on payday, or discount codes on my favourite takeaway food when I'm hungry or hungover, or a cheaper version of that thing I recently Googled but couldn't afford. Recently, I am getting heavily targeted with pregnancy tests. On their database I am a twenty-six-year-old girl with a boyfriend who has a stable job. I can't help but think we're not that far away from Facebook prying even more deeply, perhaps asking women when our periods are due each month under the category section 'Menstrual Cycle' so that they could really target us correctly with pregnancy test kits or high-end sanitary pads on the exact day of the month. Instead of filling in your date of birth, fill in the date of your next predicted period!

Now that social networks hold a scary amount of our deepest and truest information, what if a social network was to become responsible for ruining IRL relationships? What if you accidentally stumbled across something you didn't necessarily want to see online? What if the computer had more information on your 'life' than you thought?

When I first moved to London after university, in 2010, my best friend Emma and I would go out most nights. We'd drink cheap, disgusting wine at home, the type of wine that comes in a big cardboard box with a tap, and then have enough money in our pockets for one cocktail each and some pound coins for shots to see us through the night. This time, we ventured out in our glad rags to the Winchester pub in Islington, and went straight to the bar to order a radioactive-looking French Martini.

I met someone that night. I'm embarrassed to admit the way it all started: he'd overheard me say to my friend I couldn't taste the difference between Amaretto and Cointreau (I mean, to me they are the same thing) as I took a sip of the shot she'd just ordered me. I heard a mock gasp behind me and turned around and came face to face with a torso. I looked up at a very tall, smiling man peering down at me. I noticed he had a really good chin.

'Sorry to butt in, ladies. But you cannot admit to not knowing the difference between two of the most iconic liqueurs. That's ridiculous.'

The way he pronounced the word 'ridiculous' led me to believe he was a posh City boy who worked as an investment banker. Yes, I was judgemental when it came to men in pink shirts. (FYI: if he were wearing red trousers that would have been a step too far.)

'I'm Reggie, by the way.'

'Hi, Reggie.'

'I've been drinking since 4 p.m.'

'Okay.'

'What to know why?'

'Why?'

'My mate's last day at our company.' He pointed over to a bald man who was doing the Worm on the dance floor. 'He's going to another investment banking firm.' Oh God. I guessed his career correctly from his shirt.

He kept buying me different shots of both until I 'understood the difference' between the two flavours, so unsurprisingly that happened to be about twenty shots later, at which point I was slurring and hugging everyone in the bar, full of Cointreau. Or was it Amaretto? I didn't care. My friend had also paired off with someone, and I found myself stumbling back to my flat with Reggie in tow.

That was the first time he stayed at my flat and all I had was a mattress on the floor as I'd only just moved in – but it wasn't long before he started buying his own food and putting it in my fridge, very much making himself at home and coming round a lot.

I was so inexperienced with grown-up men that I thought that him coming over to my flat at 2 a.m. for a booty call was somehow romantic. I was still young enough to not suffer from hangovers so I'd let him come over in the middle of the night after his drunken work nights out, stay the night and then leave again in the morning with a very nonchalant goodbye after we'd both had about three hours' sleep. I thought we were a proper 'thing' and I enjoyed his company and relished showing my friends secret pictures I'd taken of him on my phone. He was extremely good-looking – think a young Jon Hamm. I'd secretly love the fact that he'd go up to my balcony in the mornings and sit there in his boxers eating cereal with the sun shining on his face and I'd love it if my housemate or any of her friends staying would catch sight of him too. It was shallow but I was so smug about my new 'catch'.

A few weeks later he went quiet, and I went on his Facebook page and saw he'd uploaded a Facebook photo album called 'IBIZA WITH THE GIRL'. I was confused.

I texted him: 'Hi – you have a girlfriend? Just saw on Facebook? Huh?'

He replied two days later, saying: 'Oh yes sorry forgot we were FB friends we're back together forgot to mention it don't worry and take care.'

Forgot to mention it? Don't worry? Take care?

Oh my God. I *knew* I shouldn't have trusted someone who never used punctuation in texts.

I typed out a text: 'You can't just rent my vagina for special occasions like a tuxedo!' then I deleted it. Well, actually I didn't get to send it because my friend snatched my phone away.

This is just one example of social media opening my eyes to the truth. Most of the time I didn't go looking for it. Shit would just unfold right in front of my eyes. If I hadn't seen Reggie's photos on Facebook, would he ever have told me? Or perhaps he would have carried on as normal and continued coming round to my house during the night?

The incident with Reggie wasn't the first time I found out more than I'd bargained for on social networks, I'm sad to say. I'd already had experience in that department.

It was July 2008: I'd just come home from university for the long summer break. It was that weird time of the year when I'd pack up my things in my crummy student house and move back to my parents' house for three weeks, back in my old pink room covered in watercolour illustrations of fairies with glittering wands. I'd go from being an independent student with an independent life to needing my parents more than anything again, regressing back in autopilot mode to being a needy child. This summer break always seemed to come at the most inappropriate time, either after an argument with a friend so we wouldn't be able to reconcile our differences for a while or when I had actually started enjoying it there. Southampton University was a great place to learn – even the library had so much personality – but the city itself made me feel empty. I didn't connect with its streets or bars or parks – it wasn't home, and it wasn't London. It was just 'for now'.

I'd cram all my work into these few weeks back home, thinking I could get a scary assignment done quickly, alone in my room listening to Florence and the Machine and reflecting on my life, waiting for my crappy BlackBerry to light up with something or someone interesting to distract me. Trying to attempt last-minute essays always made me feel like it was a bad idea even trying to pretend to be an academic – plus doing an English degree temporarily destroyed my love of reading. Our English lecturers made us write essays like we were at bootcamp, screeching at us to hurry up and work faster. They were stern. They used words I didn't understand. It was difficult to answer questions. In one meeting, my course tutor asked me if I'd ever been on a diet.

'Yes, I suppose I have.'

'Good. Well, think of your work as being on a diet – you have to be committed.' I wasn't sure this was the best advice to give to a student.

I went to university because it was the done thing, and I went along with it without any real conscious thought. It was, for me and my friends at the time, just *the next step*. I had friends who decided against it who are doing just as well in their careers now and by skipping university they avoided going through the unnecessary drunken pregnancy scares or 'dirty pints' or horrendous debts or being on the receiving end of jokey baked-beans-on-toast-only cookbooks at Christmas. I can't argue that my university life wasn't important; it was *my path* and I was lucky to get the opportunity in the first place. But it is still, in Western culture, treated like a traditional badge of honour, like getting married in a Pinterest-worthy white wedding dress. Neither of these things is for everyone, and yet we are led to believe we should want what everyone else wants.

I couldn't help but think that university didn't exactly give me many tangible results or life lessons except for 'how to successfully avoid someone in a nightclub'. I would daydream about what else I could have achieved in those three years apart from spending all my money on trying not to be confused and down in the dumps. But no one can be Gwyneth in *Sliding Doors*; no one knows where their life would have gone if they had chosen a different route. However, there's one thing my friends and I had in common during our university experience, and that was the fact that we had too much free time. And that free time made us sad, anxious and unhealthy. I had too much time to think, to eat, to mope. Academia post-school isn't for everyone. Some people just want to dive in and get their hands all dirty and get educated by doing the do. Not hypothetically analysing something that evaporates into thin air by the time you get out there into the world. I spent three years talking about the doing. Discussing and debating and analysing and then forgetting. It's like when people at work *have meetings all the time*, but don't actually do anything. I felt like university was ONE BIG LONG MEETING.

Another reason I was feeling so washed out was because I'd lost quite a lot of weight the previous term. I'd been aware of it for a while but had tried to blank it out. Back at home, I'd catch sight of myself in the bathroom mirror and my face seemed pointier, greyer even. I could feel the wires in the mattress digging into my back more than before. My hip bones were aching and were sore to touch, and my tummy was rumbling. Not rumbling in a light 'ooh, it must be time for lunch' sort of way, but in a way that really vibrated against my chest. My insides were jarring against each other like snakes, bellowing unattractively. I knew exactly what it was: it was my body asking me, pleading with me, to feed it properly.

I tried hard to think of the last meal I had eaten and couldn't remember. I think I'd had a nibble at a few garlic prawns the night before and I could still taste them on the roof of my mouth. I was also lying to people about what I'd eaten. The thing with lying is, the more I did it, the better I got at it and the more alone I felt while doing it. I just wanted to curl up and switch everything off, including my brain, like the lamp beside my bed that could so easily be extinguished into darkness. I was jealous of a fucking lamp. It was the first time I'd felt like I was too exhausted to carry on pulling my body around and talking to people. I couldn't sleep either; I would toss and turn because my stomach would hurt and nothing would be comfortable except folding myself into a foetal position.

Whenever I'd experienced feelings like this before, I would laugh at how pathetic I was being because it would help me snap out of it. One thing I was good at was laughing at myself when I knew I was being hormonal. But this was the first time I couldn't even give myself a little snort under the duvet to make fun of my emotional state. I was just plain sad, and not just in a caricature 'Eeyore' way – there was no cartoon rain cloud above my head. I couldn't blame this feeling on contraception or my period. The next day I had to get out of my dressing gown and drop my parents off at the airport as they were going to visit my brother in Glasgow, pretending to be fine, making quiet chit-chat in the car. Hiding my weight and hiding my sadness under a big jumper. Suddenly I was back home and alone in the house. Alone with my computer.

Staring out into the garden. Staring at the fridge. Then staring at my computer screen. Everything was numb.

The reason I wasn't eating was because I was punishing myself. It was a quiet and secret way to feel a little bit more in control.

I had cheated on him. My first teenage boyfriend. Toby. A well-to-do guy with ginger-blond hair who wore pressed trousers. He was the first twenty-something I'd met who owned an American Express. It was awful and strange and drunken and blurry. It happened with a friend's university housemate, a boy who meant nothing and who I would never see again. I phoned Toby as soon as I opened my eyes the next day, with a hangover headache, sore legs and my friend passed out next to me. I cried down the phone, pleading that I was sorry, sorry, so sorry. My phone was so wet with tears that it stopped working halfway through the phone call.

His reaction was chilling; he sounded calm. He seemed okay with it. *He* bought *me* flowers to say sorry. It was the most messed-up thing; I did something really awful and I needed him to tell me that I'd behaved monstrously and verbally scold me, blame me, shout at me. But he did the opposite. I couldn't wrap my head around it; it was like I'd gone into NatWest, robbed the tills and then had cheers, applause and confetti while exiting with bags of stolen money. The reaction was just plain *weird*. I wanted to be reprimanded, to receive the type of dressing-down that a student gets from a stern head-teacher just before being expelled, because that is what I deserved. I should have been shut out and shouted at. Instead my head felt like mashed potato because Toby was welcoming me back with open arms and had forgiven me so quickly, stroking my hair while I sobbed.

Being forgiven so quickly had made it worse. *Did he care? Did he love me at all? Did he love me too much to process what I'd done? Was he going to have a delayed reaction? Would he later murder me in my sleep and go all Macbeth on me?* I was obviously crying out for attention, but strangely I didn't get any; he just wanted to plod on as usual and kept saying, 'Let's just forget about it,' followed by, 'Let me run you a bath.' But I hadn't done a little stupid thing like admitting I'd stolen some stud earrings from Claire's Accessories. This was bad. This was *bad person* stuff.

The morning after the 'incident', my friends were silent with me while we had breakfast in their little kitchen. All I heard was the crunching of cereal, and no eye contact was made towards me. They didn't even offer me a cup of tea. I had silent tears pouring down my face but no one gave me a hug because even though I knew they desperately wanted to, I also knew they'd briefed each other not to. I understood: they couldn't pretend to be proud of my behaviour. They'd overheard the phone call and could deduce that Toby wasn't giving me any tough love, so they felt they had to instead. They had to make me feel like shit for a few days because that's what good friends do; they are cruel to be kind, and then when you've been punished enough and learned your lesson, they scrape you up off the floor like a squashed insect.

Months later, Toby and I were trying to patch things up and attempting to place a little plaster over the wound. I'd not forgiven myself for what I had done and that's when the weight loss started to happen. It happened quickly and dramatically, and soon I didn't look like me in photos. I didn't look heaps *smaller* because my frame wouldn't budge, but I was thinner enough that people started noticing a difference. When you're normally a healthy size twelve with bouncy boobs, people notice if you're even slighty smaller. I had people saying 'Where's ya arse gone?' and 'Your hugs aren't as good any more.'

At the start of the summer holidays, I went to my best friend's twenty-first party, a sit-down meal in a restaurant by the sea in Devon and sat on a table with some friends of her other university mates that I hadn't met before. I was making polite conversation while my plate remained empty an hour into the meal. My mind was whirling around so quickly that I'd been drinking but had forgotten to eat anything. This was how it had all happened: I'd been on every diet under the sun during my teens, but forgetting to eat because my mind was distracted with a thousand thoughts was the only reason I was now vanishing away. Toby was loading up his plate for seconds. One of the girls, holding a glass of wine, looked me up and down.

'Emma! Hun!' A sloppy air-kiss hit me. 'You're not eating much!' She glanced down at my plate.

Here we go again, I thought. I laughed it off, awkwardly, reaching for the bread-basket in the middle of the table and tearing off the crusts. Plus I *hated* it when strangers call me hun.

I turned to an old school friend who had clearly been knocking back the table wine. She was slurring at me and dug her nails into my arm.

'You. Look. Fantastic. Emma. I hope you don't take this the wrong way. But that dress is FALLING off you. And, well, you look *way better.*' She leaned in, and with her wine glass at a dangerous angle and her red-wine teeth nearing my face, she whispered: 'So … go on then, *how did you do it?*' She then mimed two fingers going down her throat and made a gagging noise, subtly raising an eyebrow and waiting for an answer.

I just pushed past her, like a zombie.

I then bumped into a guy I vaguely knew on the way to the toilets. I recognised him immediately; he had wide shoulders and a confident swagger I remembered from previous encounters with him before I'd left for uni. I also remembered he had bullied me during my puppy-fat teenage years, often singling me out and embarrassing me in front of his friends. I suddenly felt a hand creep around the small of my back. He reminded me of the lad culture I had been forced to deal with in the first year of university.

'Wow … Emma, you've changed.' He looked me up and down slowly. 'Excuse my forwardness … but …' He took a massive slurp on his beer, which dribbled a little down his chin. His eyes lingered on me, as he winked while his hand moved down towards my newly bony bottom. I politely asked him to remove his hand from my body and informed him I was here with my boyfriend and that I was going to the loo because I needed to change my sanitary towel – 'I have a very, very heavy period' which was 'practically dripping down my leg'. His face dropped and he stumbled off, looking confused. I rolled my eyes and pushed past him.

These reactions to my weight-loss were all very interesting to me. I had become temporarily thin for a few months (literally, a few months) and yet people were already acting so differently towards me. Not my close friends, but the acquaintances around me in the room. They suddenly seemed more interested in me because I'd drunk the skinny juice, even though I was actually the most boring person in the room because I was so hungry and tired and too busy turning down food to have fun. I could really *notice* the difference in a social environment, which was bizarre. 'Skinny Me' was attracting way more attention than 'Muffin-top Me', and it was starting to freak me out that people I knew could be so shallow. It was as if they thought I was deserving of a round of applause just for weighing less.

I had texts from people who I hadn't spoken to for years who got in contact with me the morning after the party, once the photos had popped up on Facebook: I was tagged in tons of photos of me dancing, hugging a friend, holding (but not eating) a cupcake.

Message 1: 'Hey girl. On a diet? Which one? x'

Message 2: 'You ok mate? Shall we grab a burger soon? You look like you need one x'

(Group) Message 3: 'Hi Skinny! It's the girls from Book club. Tell us your secrets!'

I had *attention*. People wanted to know *how I did it*. People who never noticed me before were suddenly looking at me. It made me feel good – but it started turning into a game. How many people could I get commenting on my weight loss? I began to feel more 'seen'. More in control.

The truth, however, was sad: I didn't get skinny because I had read the body-transformation pages of *Heat* magazine. I was skinny because I was unhappy.

Things were slowly getting back to normal, on the surface at least, and Toby and I had arranged to go on holiday with my family to see if we could still have fun together despite my weird eating habits and the fact that our relationship was pretty much doomed. This experience was vital for me to realise that once any cheating happens in a relationship it is officially dead. In the bin. RIP. It would never be the same again. It was my fault, but we agreed we owed it to ourselves to give it one last go. Plus, we'd already booked the bloody flights.

So there we were, a week later, out each night eating sardines by the sea in Portugal. A lovely villa with a pool, a good view of the sea and huge looming palm trees that gave us all a bit of shade. You could pick lemons, figs and avocados from the trees. The air was thin and hot and smelled of the tropical foliage and flowers. We'd dress up for dinner, everyone taking a longer shower, slapping after-sun on the burnt bits and putting on their nicest clothes with a spritz of their most expensive special-occasion perfume. I wore maxi dresses, even though I hated maxi dresses. I wouldn't even remember buying them. Maxi dresses would just appear every time I went on a holiday.

My family had taken a shine to Toby but I always got the feeling they knew it was a young romance, destined for a few immature dramas and potentially not lasting very long. He always wore a crisp designer shirt, had a good head of hair and could always fix a technical problem. I felt constantly sick in my stomach, but we were good at covering up the problematic undertones. I was still dealing with digesting my guilt, so I'd project emotions onto him and start to become paranoid that he would soon cheat on me, when in reality it was just because I was insecure about the fact I had. That's why people say that if you're in a relationship with someone who keeps pestering you about whether you're being unfaithful it's because they probably are. Reverse psychology and all that.

One evening we were cooking an outdoor barbecue, marinating the chicken and dancing to an iPod playlist while drinking beers. Toby was typing on his laptop but he quickly put it away and started spinning me around, taking my hand and twirling me around by the pool. I felt so distant from him – like I was on holiday with a stranger.

Later on that night, after we'd fallen asleep in a drunken blur, I awoke, stuck to his chest, peeling my clammy body away from his.

We had forgotten to the put the air-con on, and I felt my tongue had dried up like a lizard's so I decided to get water from the bathroom tap. As I got up, I noticed his laptop still whirring on the floor next to me, a small light flashing. I don't know why I thought this was a good idea but I decided to take it into the bathroom, perch on the edge of the closed toilet seat and see what the browser history said. My paranoia had reached a new level; I wouldn't normally have dreamed of touching his possessions. But he'd left the laptop on the floor, open, seemingly because he hadn't finished what he'd needed to do on it early in the night. It was too hard to resist looking.

There was nothing incriminating in his message chat, on Facebook or on Gmail, and it didn't look as though he'd been downloading any strange porn.

Click. I went onto the last site he'd visited. A Facebook page belonging to one of his friends, James, who I'd met a few times at various parties.

Click. Scrolling through James's wall was a message from another friend, Mike: 'Bloody mental night last Thursday, mate. Still reeling. Nice to see you too @Toby.'

I didn't know they'd gone out that night. Toby had told me he was with family in Surrey. *Click.* I found myself on Mike's page. On his wall were some photos featuring a lot of Toby's friends. I clicked on the album.

Scroll. Unsurprisingly Toby was in a lot of the photos, mostly hovering in the background looking a bit sweaty and lost.

Click. In all the photos, Toby was next to or drunkenly hugging a guy called Ollie.

Click. I went onto Ollie's profile – we weren't 'Friends' but he was tagged in the photo and his page was set to public so I could see everything.

Scroll. Ollie had uploaded two photo albums from the previous night. Toby was in two of the photos but he wasn't tagged, which is probably why I hadn't seen them.

I went through them all, clicking, scrolling, clicking and scrolling as I hunched over the laptop in the pitch-black bathroom, my eyes sore and swollen. I wasn't sure what I was looking for, but I was down the rabbit hole, so confused in my real life that I thought the online world might offer a few clues as to what I should do next.

Nerves were tightening in my stomach as I dug deeper into the Facebook web of friend connections.

Click. A photo of them all at the bar with their thumbs up. *Click.* A photo of James getting a kebab and laughing. *Click.* Toby giving Ollie a piggy-back in the middle of a road. *Click.* The last photo threw me. It was a picture of Toby in bed with a girl. I hovered over her face with the cursor. She was tagged as Kim.

I went onto Kim's profile, moving through her profile photos at lightning speed. *Click, click, click.* She wasn't conventionally attractive, I thought, and obviously I was looking for ways I could dismiss her as being awful – it was the middle of the night, and I was hurt. One thing I could tell from scanning through the photos, though, was that she looked really good fun. Her head was thrown back laughing in every single picture. My hand was sweating over the keypad. *Maybe I wasn't fun any more?*

In the photo, Toby was topless. He looked flustered and his hand was in her lap under the duvet. She was in her bra, looking smug. Laughing. Looking guilty. Looking straight at the camera. A definite glint in her eye.

It was the new 'looking through texts' except I wasn't just looking at some messages directly sent to him, I'd actively gone searching through seven different Facebook profiles to end up on this photo that made me feel sick. How could I explain how I'd found this photo, through a trail of people I'd never met? How could I bring this up without looking like a total psycho?

I did what any insecure human being would do next. I went through all of Kim's photos.

Afterwards, I somehow staggered back into the bedroom and fell asleep, waking up a couple of hours later with the sunshine streaming in through the window blinds. I'd had a vivid dream that I'd messaged Kim:

'Hi Kim,

I've seen the photo.

Thanks for ruining everything.'

I hadn't sent this message, but I did find it in my iPhone notes. Toby rolled over and put his arm across my stomach. I felt sick and tried to sleep. I was a jealous hypocrite. The worst kind of person. No one owed me any sympathy. And yet, I had a burning ball of hatred for this girl from Facebook who'd driven the final nail into the coffin of our relationship.

The next day was awful. I couldn't escape how glum I was feeling, but we couldn't 'have it out' properly. We were in a different country together with my family and I had to just pretend not to have seen it. We were a horrible, messy, lost cause. Everything made me feel icky and I couldn't wait to be rid of it all, although the thought of being without him made me feel scared, too. It made me question whether I was thankful to Facebook for capturing the truth of what had happened despite the fact it was something I was never *meant to have seen.*

We flew back home, and it was clear he couldn't do or say the right things; it was unfixable in so many ways. I rang my best friend, Charlotte, each morning asking for reassurance: 'I need to break up with him, don't I?'

Her reply was firm but fair: 'I mean this is the nicest possible way here Em, but you've asked me the same question almost every day now for a week, I don't know what else to say that I haven't already said. Maybe the fact you keeping asking me is your answer …?'

She was right. If you keep asking someone the same question over and over, whether it's career, relationship or whatever, you are clearly unhappy, and you have to suck it up and change things yourself. Deep down you already know the answer. I stopped making myself sick. I found myself back in the arms of the people who made me feel most like me and I felt better – inside and out.

Back in the day it was so much harder to find out if someone was being unfaithful to you. People used to be unfaithful to each other all the time; we have enough literature to last a lifetime that chronicles the scandals of infidelity. Without social media you would never have had to worry unless a real-life pair of eyes had seen you sneaking around, or you were careless enough to leave a restaurant bill in your pocket or whatever.

But a photo circling the Internet? It's made it easier to find things out by accident. Though of course I didn't technically find out by accident – I went digging. It made me wonder how much we choose to see, and how much we choose to avoid. I'm sure I could find out lots more information on many things if I tried hard enough. The computer holds so many Exhibit As.

I've had friends say they've strongly suspected that their boyfriends have cheated on them while away on a gap year, and fretted

100

over whether to tell them what they'd seen. The girlfriend would see group photos emerge on Facebook with people looking a *little bit too close* and would start sussing things out. But even then you can't know the truth. At least with my situation no one had to tell me, not even Toby; I found out because someone was stupid enough to upload the evidence online. On the Internet it can be easy to stumble across things you don't necessary want to see. In this scenario, I actually did have Facebook to thank. But if you feel you have to go digging in the first place, you've already proved that something's not right, at all.

*'All men that date me have to know that their name may
end up in a pop song.'*

Ke$ha

chapter 6

Online Dating isn't the Same as Online Shopping

2010

Excuse me for generalising, but some male Internet users need serious help when it comes to personal branding on social media. Have you ever noticed that when a friend of yours has met a new male squeeze, and you ask to 'see a few piccies', they instantly clam up and say 'no, honestly, he looks *so* much better in real life'?

It's true: if you go through a early-twenty-something guy's Facebook page, you're guaranteed to find photos of one, if not all, of the following:

1. A gross photo of his mate from 2007 he put up as a joke.

2. A photo of him posing in a beer-stained fancy-dress outfit.

3. A picture taken on a dance floor in a *Saturday Night Fever* pose, him open-shirted.

4. A very, very old photo that looks nothing like him. At all.

5. A blurry pic of him passed out with a banana skin on his face.

6. A totally irrelevant cartoon.

7. Their favourite footballer or sporting hero.

This is because (I'm guessing) guys are normally a bit more chilled out about how they are presented online and probably don't strategically select to quite the extent that girls do. Unfortunately, this makes it trickier for girls to 'Facebook stalk' them before their first date, and also makes it hard for outsiders to approve of their overall aesthetic. It's important to stay open-minded, because if you took the Facebook photos at face value you'd probably never even get to the first date. The best thing, really, is to not social-media stalk them at all prior to the date. Wait for the big reveal. Like the olden days.

Let me paint you a picture of one of my very first Internet dates in London. I was twenty-one and a Twitter obsessive (still am), and occasionally people would randomly respond to my bizarre flow of 140-character consciousness, which would often lead to unplanned flirty one-liners. They'd slide into my DMs and we'd arrange to meet in real life. One sunny afternoon, I had a request for a date from a guy named Mike, a suited and booted senior advertising man I'd been in contact with for a few weeks. A digital

Don Draper, if you will. His Twitter avatar was slightly pixelated and small, but the goods were there: a full head of hair, a smart suit and a nice smile. I was also able to look at his LinkedIn profile to make sure he was telling the truth about his big-time career. Yep, he was definitely not lying. Every advertising award under the sun. As I was interning at a PR agency I thought I could use this date for two things: 1) asking nosy questions about the industry, and possibly find better job opportunities, and 2) get some dating practice in. It'd been a few months since I'd dumped Toby (even though he was still sending me the odd drunken text) but I was now ready to go on adult dates in the city. Without wanting to sound a cliché ... oh fuck it: I had Samantha Jones vibes. (Turned out that Samantha Jones gave a very unrealistic portrayal of what it meant to have a job in PR, however.)

The private message had popped up while I was at work.

'Hey you. Wanna go for dinner tomorrow after work? M.'

He then favourited four of my (self-proclaimed) hilarious tweets.

I agreed to meet up with him. After all, Mike looked harmless. And I had just moved to London, coincidentally, at a time when my libido was sky-high. At the time I was reading Dawn O'Porter's *Diaries of an Internet Lover* and, compared to her threesomes, old men and jaunts abroad, my life seemed embarrassingly dull. I was in the Big Smoke! Young, free and single! Living with my best mate in our very own bachelorette pad! Most of my team-mates at work were in relationships or married so I thought I'd do them a favour and let them live vicariously through me. Yes, that is how narcissistic and self-involved I was at twenty-one. That's what the Internet does to you. I was certain that the rest of my shared desk couldn't wait to hear about my most recent date like it was the first sentence of a new Harry Potter book.

Ever since Mike had first been in contact with me, I had started to really look forward to receiving his messages, especially after a gruelling day at my PR internship, in which the strange tasks included going to M&S's lingerie section to buy my boss some stick-on chicken fillets to go under her strapless dress that she'd just ordered from ASOS. Obviously, I'd already found Mike on Facebook and LinkedIn, meaning that I had gone through his entire backlog of life milestones. My aim was to investigate the following:

1. Hobbies: either interesting ones I could ask him about later on or, conversely, to discover any weird ones that could be a deal breaker for me, such as birdwatching or stamp-collecting.

2. Any topless pics: so I could suss out what lay underneath.

3. Good and bad pictures: to screenshot onto my phone to show my mates at the pub.

4. An idea of what sort of crowd he hung out with: lads? Rock-climbers? Drug-dealers?

Tapping my way through his Facebook photos I couldn't find anything particularly incriminating – in fact, all his photos were averagely lovely, all from the same angle, all with either a nice-looking mate or nice-looking family member, and it was obvious that he was really into sailing. Most photos were of him either next to, on or inside some sort of boat or object that moves through water. It was just so inoffensive. I was gutted. Firstly, it meant I had nothing funny to screen-grab on my phone to show my mates, and secondly, to me, having a vanilla online profile is the worst thing you can have. But at least it made me think he'd be safe to meet up with.

The following evening I braved the date. We decided to meet by Covent Garden tube station. I hid inside a shop just opposite and waited for him to arrive; I've always hated being 'that' person, the one who gets there first and has to pretend to check their phone awkwardly. So I started browsing aimlessly through the rails of Reiss, still managing to be in the line of sight of the station through the shop window. When I glanced back, I saw a very tall man with brown hair and a long grey coat standing on the other side of the road, looking around. He was there. He checked his phone. I held my breath and went outside to meet him.

'Mike?'

I touched his arm.

'Emma! Hey!' He air-kissed me, which I wasn't sure I liked. 'So,' he said. 'I've booked a table at the Circus, round the corner.'

'We're going to a circus?' Suddenly I felt like an idiot in my heels.

He laughed. 'No. It's a restaurant. Cabaret-themed. Let's go.'

Between mouthfuls of posh food, we were interrupted by an occasional bum-cheek shaking in our faces. This restaurant was indeed 'cabaret-themed', which I was not opposed to in principle, but what I didn't realise was that every fifteen minutes they dimmed the lights so that you could not locate your knife and fork and then *on top of* your table appeared your very own individual performer. It was an ice-breaker, that's for sure – but it was also slightly intense, given the fact that we'd essentially both just seen a drag queen's pubic hair before dessert.

We talked about films, music and careers, trying to ignore the fact that on the table next to us there was a couple discussing getting divorced. It was the usual first-date kind of chat. I find myself being quite good at covering most bases on dates; I seem to have a minimal amount of knowledge of pretty much anything, when really I'm just blagging my way along. Shout out to Barbara Walters's classic book *How to Talk with Practically Anybody about Practically Anything*. No awkward silences here. I had a perfectly pleasant time.

Mike and I went on a few more dates. One date consisted of us, oddly, going to the local library. He arrived at the pub and slammed a library card down on the table: 'You said you liked reading!' So off we went, finding ourselves a corner in the library café with coffee and croissants. But it turned bit stale and we ended up reading through a rogue *Hello*! magazine while rather flatly discussing celebs, the London housing crisis and how much Lord Sugar's anti-wrinkle eyelid surgery must have cost him. I let some yawns slip out of my mouth, but he didn't catch on.

This date dragged on for seven hours (post-library we went for lunch, then cinema, dinner, nightcap, then a late-night ice-cream shop). My friend was texting me: 'Do the cash machine trick!' But I let the date go on, and on, so I could definitely be sure: yes, I definitely wasn't into Mike. Conversationally. Or sexually. Maybe it was the fact that we'd exchanged a few flirty texts messages in which he kept calling my boobs 'breasts'.

I started replying that I was 'super busy at work!' and made up that 'my sister is really unhappy at the moment, so she's coming to stay'. My sister was actually living it up at university, in her freshers' year, and couldn't have been happier, but I was just praying he wouldn't try to Facebook-stalk her for proof. As time went on, he started getting a bit aggravated with me for avoiding meeting up in real life.

Then came the Facebook message essays.

Hi Emma,

I just wanted to get in touch because I'm sort of getting the impression that you don't want to go out on any more dates with me. I'm just a bit confused, and I'm disappointed really that you'd just not be honest with me about this.

The thing is, I've spent quite a lot of time (and money!) organising the dates for us, and well, I thought they were going really well. I thought we were getting on really well.

I know you're a lot younger than me, but how you're handling this is very immature. I find it really fucking annoying actually, when girls do this to guys. We make such an effort, trying to impress you, wine and dine you, and then when you get bored or scared, you just hack off out of it, giving no explanation.

You've made me feel like you like me by texting me so much in between dates and us kissing the other night after we had that frozen yoghurt. You're giving me proper mixed signals and it's really not on. What you're doing is pretty harsh, Em, and if I'm the first guy to point this out to you – then, so be it.

Well, I guess the reason for this message is because I'm asking you for an explanation. Be a grown-up and tell me what is going on.

Thanks,

M

I felt there were so many things wrong with this. I screamed, and took my laptop into my best mate's room, reading the message aloud like I was on stage in the West End.

'Am I harsh? Am I harsh, really? Tell me if I'm being harsh,' I said. I was feeling dramatic, not to mention weirded out. I pointed to my laptop screen, demanding that my best friend read his message in full.

'You're not being harsh. This guy is getting weird,' my housemate said, walking into the kitchen to check on her chocolate brownies.

Here's our WTF list that we decided on, together:

1. Facebook is not the medium to write long-winded passive-aggressive essays to someone you've gone on four dates with.

2. I don't think it's okay to shame a girl into going on more dates with you.

3. I didn't *ask* for Mike to pay for the dinners, he insisted. Anyway, I was a broke intern, whereas he had a full-time, well-paid job, so it seemed fair enough.

Thankfully, this was before that updated version of Facebook messages where a little tick appears to show that you have read it. He didn't know that I'd seen it, so they kept on coming. The first message was quickly followed by another, simultaneously more angry and more formal.

Dear Emma,
I trust you got my message??

I'm just following up with you, to check you received it and your thoughts on the matter.

As you can tell, I'm just a bit hurt, to be honest, by your actions. We've spent a long time together now, and I just wanted you to be clear with me.

Thanks to you and your previous interest in me, or so it seemed, I'd actually told my mum that we were pretty much official. For me to tell my mum I had a girlfriend, that's quite serious. I thought you wanted that. I really want this to work out. I think I'd make a good boyfriend for you. What do you think?

I haven't had this connection with anyone for a while. I'm serious about this. Also, I'm nearly thirty, so I need to find someone.

Please write back and let me know what the situation is. For my mum, at least.

M

I replied once, saying I was sorry but I just wasn't in the right headspace at the time to start having a proper relationship. The truth was that this whole exchange gave me the creeps; I always think that if there are any warning signs in the very few weeks of getting together with someone you know to back slowly away. In the words of my best friend: 'If they are irritating during the honeymoon period then *imagine* what they'll be like five years into the relationship. This is meant to be the *fun* bit.'

The good thing about the Internet is you can just delete people from your personal spaces. 'Out of sight, out of mind' can actually be true (the modern version, of course, is 'out of newsfeed, out of mind'). It's not nice to admit, but once I removed a girl from university from Facebook and then genuinely forgot she existed until I bumped into her years later in WHSmith. Often, we don't tend to think about people now unless we have some sort of visual prompt. Which is why it's dangerous to have your Facebook newsfeed set on 'Top Stories', as Facebook chooses what is most relevant to you. Having your settings on 'Most Recent' means you can pick what you want to interact with.

After I had managed to distance myself enough from Mike for him to have finally removed me from Facebook (cue a sigh of relief), I decided to explore a few other avenues. Mainly, those 'other avenues' were the dating websites advertised on public transport, normally featuring a guy with a terrifyingly white smile who was perched on the edge of a picnic bench with a bunch of roses looking lovingly into the camera.

London is known for being the type of city that can leave you feeling lonely in a crowded room because it is bloody hard to meet decent people. It's not difficult to find *people* in general – they're everywhere – but it is difficult to find people you wouldn't mind spending a rainy Sunday afternoon with.

Guardian Soulmates was recommended to me by a friend who said she'd had some recent success with it. This roughly translated into the fact that she'd gone on a few dates via the website without being forced to say she was 'going to the cash machine' in order to run away to the tube station with her coat over her head. This site was clearly for 'young professionals', or people whose entire identity and ego is apparently formed around what type of job they have. The website was basically the dating version of LinkedIn because it was *all* about your profile, and your professionalism – and it was mostly frequented by men in suits. It was like being at a dinner party when your friend's parents lean in, their glasses perched on the end of their nose, asking, 'And what do you do?' Every single message I received – at the time, you could receive messages for free, but in order to reply you had to pay the membership fee – asked me about my career, and seeing as I didn't actually have a full-time job back then, it was making me feel a bit rubbish.

I'm sure it's been updated since 2010, but filling out your profile on Guardian Soulmates took a while, and by that I mean an *entire afternoon*. I knew I didn't have the cash to join up, but I used the profile system to practise writing my bio and fill out my interests. I was surprised at the sort of things Internet dating sites asked, such as your 'body type' from a drop down menu of 'slim, average, athletic or rather not say', especially as they were being viewed publicly. The robots behind Guardian Soulmates wanted you to put enough data and material into the system as possible in order for them to set you up with a 'soulmate match'. The more they knew, the more scarily accurate they could be. However, the questions the robots asked you could become quite personal at times. I started to feel like the only person who knew more about me than the Guardian Soulmates robots was my gynaecologist. Hair colour was the starting point: you could pick from 'black', 'blonde', 'brown' or 'grey' (followed by the inevitable 'joke' about whether the collar matches the cuffs, usually made by men called Gary who work in accounts).

The website also asked you exactly where you were born; your nationality; your relationship status (I mean, hopefully it's single?); education level (is this a job interview?); whether you smoke (do I tell the truth?); drinking (whether it's 'excessive' or 'a few a week' – bit nosy); religion; whether you have kids and whether you want kids in the future. So basically, if you printed out the dating site form and put it next to your GP's notes, or your census response, you wouldn't be able to tell the difference. I felt like I was accidentally applying for a mortgage when the 'how much do you (CONFIDENTIALLY) earn each year?' questions started popping up.

I didn't mind filling all of this out, of course, but it was difficult to tailor your answers. For example, on the 'do you smoke?' question, the only options were 'never', 'occasionally' or 'regularly' (nowadays it should include an e-cigarettes option for those who like to 'vape' – maybe it does). I sort of wish they'd included a little box underneath that allowed you to elaborate on each question, so that you could type out an optional essay. I would have added a footnote for sure: 'Well, actually I guess I'd call myself a social smoker. Yes, that is a proper thing and not a bullshit phrase that hardcore addicts use to lie to their doctors (and to themselves). And I'm trying to give up anyway because when I *really* think about it, I get freaked out at what it's doing to my skin. So if you smoke, please don't offer me any. If you don't smoke, don't be put off, I have broken all my twenty-packs in half which are currently lying at the bottom of my bin. Let's talk either way.' I wanted to be able to expand so I could further explain and justify the boxes I'd ticked, and thought that doing so would be beneficial in courting my new potential partner, because then they would be fully briefed on the backstory and where I was at psychologically. I couldn't understand the idea that ticking some extremely limited multiple-choice boxes would be a good way to meet my future partner. I felt like just another number in the machine.

The next stage was the photo uploads. Your chance to show the world your best selfies. The advice from the robots was this: 'Make your photo bright and clear, in portrait style, and show personality.' Showing personality was translated by many users as holding a pint with a thumbs-up, a cheesy grin and a wink to suggest 'I like to swig Jägermeister out the bottle and move my hips like Olly Murs!' Showing personality is always difficult in one photo. It can often result in being a bit over the top. It made me think that many people should upload a short video instead like they were applying for *Big Brother*.

Next on the checklist was a little box for you to 'share your story', by creating your own personalised introduction. This was the online equivalent to *Blind Date*'s 'what's your name and where do you come from?' section. The robots had some more advice here: 'Our tips are to be honest, be human and be specific – think about how you might start a conversation.' BE HUMAN? Well, I'm glad you gave me that advice, robots, because I was going to pretend to bark like a dog at this stage of the process, in a desperate attempt to get the conversation going.

The intriguing thing about these dating websites is how they make their money. It's understandable: this dating service is a business. So for £96 every six months, you can do the following: see more pictures of people (swiping through a gallery), unlimited messaging, advanced search options (searching for all sorts of niche requirements, perhaps: 'thirty-one years old, silver fox'), or find qualities you both have in common ('likes picnics, allergic to cats'). But, and excuse me for being old-fashioned, do you remember when falling in love came for FREE? Imagine having to dig into your pocket every time you got chatting at the bar with a potential date, having to hand over a tenner for every question or every reply to a question. The price tag put me off because as an intern I was earning an embarrassingly low wage. After my rent and bills I remember being left with £50 to last the whole month. There were even times when I couldn't afford to top up my own Oyster card to get the tube *into work* (oh, the crippling, tragic irony), so it seemed a bit extravagant to fork out on these Prince Charming-seeking robots. I didn't even have £100 to my name. As this premium dating site wasn't an option, I realised I was going to have to find him on foot. Or at least try some cheaper, less intense dating sites first. So I typed in 'free online dating' into my friend Google to see what my options were.

I was only three clicks away from landing on Plenty of Fish ('The Leading Free Online Dating Site', according to them), also known as the poor man's Guardian Soulmates. I managed to dive straight in, as the sign-up process was extremely simple; it didn't have the same meticulous robot gatekeepers that guarded the entrance to Soulmates. Nor was it just a service for young professionals: it was for literally *anybody* with a keyboard and a brain cell. So within ten minutes of being 'live', my inbox was out of control with new messages, rolling in by the minute, from people with usernames such as SCARY_STU with a blurred-out profile picture and messages such as 'aight bird? wht u 2' or quite simply 'wana fuk?' Or my favourite: 'i'm having a party and you and my dick are invited.'

I didn't want to 'fuk' anyone. I wanted to find a nice boy who was maybe reading a Haruki Murakami novel. I wanted to have a discussion about his favourite cafés; or to find out whether he was more of a coffee or tea person; or whether he was good at cooking roast dinners. The type of conversation I was getting hit up with daily on POF was not intellectually stimulating or interesting at all. I was just getting daily messages from guys in backwards caps asking if I would send them 'some nudez'. I had never in my life sent a nude picture, even to my previous boyfriend, and I was not going to start doing it to random lads posing topless in their bathroom mirror, covered in bling and tattoos of boobs. I started getting really disheartened.

Until I got chatting to Fred.

Fred was a guy who made me laugh from his first message:

Hey Emma. I'm new to this online dating thing. Not sure how to start off a convo really. I guess what I'm trying to say is, I read your profile and you sound cool. I've seen some pretty dire things on here … and your profile made me laugh. I could go for the cocky alpha-male Joey-From-Friends approach and do a 'what's cooking good-looking' chat-up line thing OR I could tell you that I work in a bookshop and wear a waistcoat, a bit like that skinny guy in Richard Curtis's Notting Hill. (But I'm blond and don't have a ginger beard.) I'd love to chat more. Let me know if you fancy it. No pressure, though.

I was immediately relieved to receive a normal message from someone who wasn't a sleazy man addressing me as some variation of an egg-laying vertebrate (honestly: the amount of "sup chick?', 'aight bird?' or 'what's up duck?' I had endured). Being the romanticising bookworm that I am, we instantly clicked and he told me funny stories about his days working in an independent bookshop near London Fields. His photo was a headshot, passport-style: chiselled cheekbones, piercing eyes. Mercifully, he was also wearing clothes. I managed to work out a way to block most incoming messages, except for Fred's. I went from hating the website enough that I considered deleting it to downloading the app onto my phone so I could immediately see when Fred's messages came in.

One afternoon in the pub, my friend Liv asked me why I was grinning so much at my phone.

'You know that guy I mentioned a while ago? The one I said works in the Hackney bookshop? Well, we've been messaging for ages now. He's ... cool.' I grin some more.

'Let's see a pic, then?'

I showed Liv the one photo I had of Fred saved on my phone, which I'd screen-grabbed and saved onto my camera roll. 'Here.' I shoved my phone onto her lap.

Liv's face turned pink as she locked eyes with my phone. Her lip was twitching.

'Mate. This picture.' Livvi tapped on the screen and looked at me with a serious face. 'This is a picture of quite a well-known male model. It's a picture of Pixie Lott's boyfriend. Think he's called Oliver Cheshire.'

'WHAT?' I snatched back my phone.

'Yeah. That's definitely a picture of him.' Liv is very on point with her celebrity knowledge. She's also constantly got her nose stuck in *Hello!* and *OK!* and I did not for one second doubt this information was correct.

'Oh God,' I inhaled sharply. 'So, does this mean that Pixie Lott's boyfriend is chatting to me even though he is in a relationship with a famous singer? Am I his bit on the side?'

Liv threw back her head and cackled. 'NO, Emma. This means that someone has stolen a picture of Pixie Lott's boyfriend from Google and is using it as his profile photo on Plenty of Fish to woo people. Fred is a FAKE. People steal pictures from Google all the time. In fact, I've seen this exact picture of him being used elsewhere before on dating sites. It's probably one of the first things that comes up when people search 'male model'.

I turned bright red. It all made sense. I couldn't believe, after all this time and especially since I was the one who caught out Gwen's catfishing episode, that I was still so naive.

I went home and logged onto Fred's profile to try and 'out' him as a fake. As the page loaded, a message suddenly came up: 'This account has been suspended.' Under the website rules, one of the top reasons for account suspension was for faking or impersonating anyone in your profile.

So I admit it, I totally failed with online dating during my early twenties. For someone so supposedly 'Internet savvy', I just couldn't seem to pick the right people, or take the right risks, or believe in the system enough. I would get upset and annoyed by the boxes I had to put myself into, or the funny one-liners I had to deliver to get anyone to talk to me. I hated trying to be 'quirky' or feeling like I had to upload a picture of me wearing a rollneck, scarf and mittens in order to deter the sex pests. I hated the fact that you were essentially part of an online cattle market with people judging you on the basis of three photos and then deciding if you were worth it. (Tinder didn't exist at that point but it's the same premise, and I still don't quite see how one can swipe 'yes' or 'no' based on just one photo of someone.)

This was another reason I hated nightclubs, because it's basically just an environment designed for two things to happen: 1) for strangers to dry-hump on a dance floor, or 2) for strangers to actually hump back at someone's house. It is no environment to chat or meet a life partner or talk about real topics. I know friends who met in a club and are now married, but it was something I could only see as the rare exceptions to the rule. In a dark nightclub you are in an aesthetic competition with everyone else in the room. Everyone is trying to attract a mate. To me, a dating website was just as depressing as a badly lit nightclub in Magaluf with a sweaty DJ playing Rihanna's 'Rude Boy'.

I also hated that you only got a limited number of photos to upload to 'show your personality' because none of them would be able to do that. I didn't like how strategic you had to be. ('Right. I'll upload this photo of me at this festival, so he knows I'm into music, and I'm FUN, and I can dance and that I have tons of mates!') I would put up pictures of myself fully clothed, smiling in a coffee shop, or wearing a massive scarf in the middle of a country walk, or in an art gallery trying to look cultured, but I wouldn't receive any messages. Then, as a test, I would pick the photos from me at university, during the months I made myself sick, wearing a 'going-out top' that showed off my jutting collarbones and bronzed cleavage – and the messages would roll in. The predictability depressed me. Gross.

Maybe I was doing it completely wrong, but the idea of picking your new boyfriend off the Internet, like selecting a new pair of shoes from ASOS, never truly appealed to me. I was able to make incredible friends through social networking sites, but that was always an organic, natural development over weeks or months of chit-chat back and forth, building up a friendship over time, with no agenda. When it came to dating men online, I never felt comfortable meeting up with strangers who would hint towards a 'Netflix and Chill' situation while forcing the conversation because we had zero common interests despite the algorithms. I found it difficult having no mutual friends to discuss; there was no 'oh cool, you know Smithy too – he's a hoot!' icebreaker. And I was always petrified they would be disappointed when meeting up with me in person, because most of the time I would look better in the photos.

So I went back to basics, deleted all of my online dating apps and swore I'd never go on one again. I decided I would either be single forever or meet someone one day in the grocery store like all those cheesy American rom-coms (think Bradley Cooper and Scarlett Johansson in *He's Just Not That into You*). Neither of these things happened. But I'm still glad I deleted online dating from my life.

Over the ensuing years I have found that using social media helps me to meet new people who I later end up dating, but entering environments that were strictly used for dating did nothing positive for me. Twitter and Instagram are now brilliant for hook-ups because you're in an environment that is just about communicating with everyone rather than solely potential partners.

Dating sites had made me hide behind a screen more and go out less, making excuses to stay indoors so I could scan through faces. Instead I needed opportunities to talk to people in real life. I would pester my friends to step up their match-making game because I believed that if their eligible friends-of-friends were introduced to me more often I wouldn't be having this crisis in the first place. '*Host more dinner parties*,' I'd cry to my loved-up friends, 'but not cringe ones where it is boy-girl-boy-girl and you all have to play guess the Post-it note on my head!' I would beg my friends to come out with me so I could meet more single people in nice chilled-out environments.

In fact, I met my boyfriend Paul in 2011 because a mutual colleague of ours decided to throw impromptu drinks on the roof of her flat near Buckingham Palace. We sat up there, a big group of us, drinking wine, and I looked up from my dating apps long enough to realise that I had *really* taken a shine to someone standing in front of me. Then I stalked him both in real life and online, and Facebook and Google chat helped us get things going IRL.

The world has finally got to grips with Internet dating being an actual thing that isn't weird or new any more. In fact, the opposite is true now: if you announce you have met someone naturally in real life there is a gasp, and a 'wow!' response. How on earth did you manage to meet someone you like *in person*? Dating apps have evolved in such a way that you can find people within a tiny radius, so you can search for single people near you. In fact, the search tools are getting more and more hyper-localised, so soon you'll probably be able to search within a metre's distance, meaning you'll just need an app to ask out one of the three people standing next to you at a pub bar, or the dude you see every morning on your train platform. The app will say: 'The person standing right next to you is single.' Really, deep down, we *know* that we don't need to go via an app to get permission to ask someone on a date. We've been initiating romance in person for thousands of years. But now our phones are acting as our agents. Our middlemen. Our don't-shoot-the-messenger.

When my nan and granddad met, it was at a village dance during the war. When my granddad wanted to see her again he had to cycle miles to her door (and hope he remembered the way). For us always-connected millennials, the very idea of having to do that in order to connect with another human being is mind-blowing. By contrast, we swipe people left and right, treating potential partners like they are T-shirts in a Topshop sale.

In America, more than a third of new marriages now start online, which is a fair chunk of people. It's changed everything. Casual dating sites are now so engrained in our everyday vocabulary that apps now act as both a verb and a noun: 'No he's not my boyfriend, just a Tinder!' or 'I'm going to Plenty of Fish it up this weekend!' I have been at the pub with male work friends who swipe continuously while talking to you, looking you in the eye and nodding, all the while inconspicuously moving their thumb to the left, to the left.

Now that I am in a long-term relationship, I am out of the dating scene. Even though it was great that deleting my dating apps meant I could free up space on my iPhone for other things like the Domino's delivery app, I'd often become jealous of friends who were off to meet up with strangers, as it was the random connections of online dating that I missed. Most of the time, I'd enjoy the experience more than the person. Being a writer and a nosy person I remember almost hoping for a really terrible, awkward date because it would make an entertaining blog post (I refer you to Nora Ephron's famous belief that 'everything's copy', or Caitlin Moran's advice that things fall into two categories: 'brilliant experiences and awful experiences which will later make amazing anecdotes').

I certainly had a rough time with online dating. I think one of your tasks in life (whether you're in a perfectly smug relationship or not) is to take the initiative to introduce two of your single friends from different social circles who you think could hit it off. Or host impromptu informal gatherings. Or any real-life things! I know we treat our phones like lovers but let's not treat real-life dating like it's an endangered species. It's not dead yet. Let's at least try and keep it alive.

'No woman gets an orgasm from shining the kitchen floor.'

Betty Friedan

chapter 7
Nice Porn, for Nice People

2009

Harriet and I were sitting one evening in the Firehouse Exeter, getting through a tasty £5 bottle of red wine and smoking roll-up cigarettes like we usually did on a Friday night in our home town. Nights like this normally consisted of us sitting in the corner, wearing huge scarves that covered half our faces and trying to avoid conversations with any past flames or acquaintances from the year below us at school.

While Harriet got up to go to the loo I checked my phone – and an advert for a hardcore porn site popped up as I opened my browser, out of the blue, uninvited. I stared at it. I was glued to it. How could something so graphic hit me off guard like that, when I was sitting in a pub that was playing relaxing smooth jazz in the background? Had I drunkenly Googled this? A big veiny action man was leaning over a blonde girl with drawn-on eyebrows, who looked like she was having the worst time ever. She was smiling at the camera, but it was clear she was also subtly rolling her eyes. Her stare was vacant.

It rattled my emotions mainly because I didn't expect to see it but also because I felt a sadness for the girl's vacant expression, perhaps because I could relate to her. I had been in that position – not on a porn set but in real life, having sex with someone in a way I wasn't comfortable with. I'm sad to say that my younger self did 'go along with it' at times, which now makes me shake my grown-up head in disappointment at how insecure I must have been. I closed the advert and shuddered. Maybe it was the memories it brought back of having that same expression myself during the act, or maybe it was simply because I am an emotional being, but I couldn't help but think, '*Is she all right? Where's her cardigan?*' Of course, a lot of women enjoy this line of work, but in this particular video, it looked so forced – and that jarred with me.

Technically, every time you hide an ad, especially inside a social network, it *should* send an alert so that you don't get it repeated again. That's the way it should work, so that you have some sort of control over what you see and don't see in your personal news-feeds. I mentally crossed my fingers that I wouldn't get any other porno adverts while I was, say, relaxing at my boyfriend's nan's house pre-Sunday roast or during an important meeting with my boss.

Harriet came back from the loo, clutching a new bottle of red, and sat back down. I couldn't help but bring up my dilemma, while topping up both our glasses.

'Why does porn upset me so much?' I sighed, putting my phone back down on the table, pushing it away from me.

She didn't need any context or an explanation. 'Because it's all one-sided!' Harriet lit a cigarette. 'And why is it always two extremes? From what I've seen, it's either some sloppy kissing to bad music or something that resembles a gory horror film.'

'If I went onto porn sites regularly I think I'd never have sex again,' I say, seriously.

'I agree. Where's the fun stuff for your average twenty-something woman? I think there's a gap in the market, genuinely.'

'Shall we make our own site? We could call it NotTooGrim. com.'

'Ha. I'm not sure I'm ready to change careers into being a porn director. But I really hope someone does.'

'There must be an alternative …'

'Yeah, I really wish there was somewhere we could go online that would get us in the mood, without it being so gross that it scars you for life. We're lacking stuff from the woman's point of view.'

'Like SlightlyMoreRealisticPorn.com or NothingTooExtreme. co.uk?'

'Or LittleBitofPornAfterAFewDrinks.com?'

We were getting hysterical. We brainstormed, laughed, drank wine and wrote down our ideas on napkins. Our issue was that there simply didn't seem to be any destinations for young women among the main porn sites that offered any real alternatives to the classic male fantasies, or that didn't have strange fake message chats popping up, informing you about 'milfs in your area'.

The comedian Tania Edwards once compared porn to WWF wrestling 'because everyone knows it's not real and still pretends to enjoy it'. Where's the stuff that isn't just made with a certain type of man in mind? Where's the stuff for adventurous women, made by women? Where's the stuff for non-adventurous women? What about the people who don't want anything too niche or XXX rated? As a pair of twenty-something women, we sat discussing how we couldn't help but just feel *really left out*. It was as though all the men in the world were having a secret party, slapping their penises out, and they were in charge of all the porn in the world. A big old boys' club. Where were the women's thoughts or feedback? Where could we pitch ideas?

Of course, this is the case with every other industry; it's not porn-specific. *Where can women pitch ideas?* is an age-old question. The movie industry is just as bad: the annual 'Celluloid Ceiling' report found women directed only 7 per cent of the 250 top-grossing films in Hollywood in 2014, which means a whopping 93 per cent were directed by men. It's not just about porn, but sex is important, and if we can't see a whole host of different people and situations and environments reflected back at us, then we'll keep feeling like women's sexuality doesn't matter.

Porn itself, as a thing, is not the issue, but the porn *industry* is the questionable bit. Sex sells. We all love sex. As Cindy Gallop, founder of MakeLoveNotPorn.com, says, you can be 'pro-porn, pro-sex and pro-knowing the difference'. I have absolutely nothing against anyone who chooses to work in that industry, and I like the *idea* of porn. In fact, I think that's why I feel so let down by it. For me it's the same feeling as going to my local cinema and seeing that there's nothing I like on.

When women are in charge of at least half of porn of videos being made, I think everyone would benefit. 'Role play' scenes would be much less cringey. A range of diverse women would be featured. We'd share our porn favourites over email. We'd share curated playlists. We'd have porn clubs instead of book clubs and discuss our latest 'finds'. It would be less stereotypical – on most porn sites, the 'women' section just features some oily massages and a few perfect blonde lesbians having a pillow fight.

Many adults are well aware that porn is not how real adults have sex; it's often a male fantasy, constructed by men. Things go a bit skewiff in real life: sometimes you've forgotten to sort out your bush; or you fall off the bed; or there's no massive *storyline*, you just really like each other, and you're having sex on an IKEA bed, following a nice wine-fuelled meal. Rarely on mainstream porn sites do you find videos of people having sex who actually look as if they like each other. Why can't we see more porn where the two people are, you know, actually in love – or at least fancy each other a bit?

I didn't discover porn properly until I was about nineteen, when some boys at university put it on after a night out, having inviting a group of people back to their room for what we thought was just 'some more drinks'. I'm glad that I'd seen enough IRL naked bodies before then to know that squeaky-clean bald-eagle vaginas and tanned, twelve-inch-long penises aren't exactly the norm. If not, I would have run for the hills and never had sex ever – in fact, I would probably have hidden under a blanket until I died, trying to hide every inch of my body that wasn't as smooth as a pebble.

But teenagers nowadays are more exposed than ever. And they are exposed early: 90 per cent of boys have seen online porn and 60 per cent of girls before they are eighteen years old, according to a study by Covenant Eyes. It is sad to think that young kids will think they are not good enough if they watch porn before receiving any realistic sex ed, especially if they are essentially watching two people as shiny as Madame Tussauds's waxworks having rough sex.

I admit that my sex life would probably benefit slightly from a little visual stimulus (after all, that's all porn is) because I'm a visual person – I would actually *like* to watch some porn that consists of REAL PEOPLE HAVING REAL AUTHENTIC SEX, a little online destination to go to with your partner, or alone. Orgasms make your skin better, get your heart-rate going, get your legs sweaty like you've been for a run. They are a bit like Bikram yoga but without the rip-off price tag or the creepy man in Speedos behind you. That's my kind of exercise. Getting sweaty while lying down horizontal. Win-win.

The 'shame' factor that comes with watching porn is real (and we don't need Michael Fassbender to remind us), especially for women. People still think female masturbation is something that should never be discussed, and it has still only been seen a handful of times on TV or in films. But what if porn was reinvented as something for everyone? What if there were multiple destinations with lots of levels for all different kinds of people, like a Mario Kart game? When Caitlin Moran was asked what she'd like the future of porn to look like, she said: 'Like ... Pinterest! You know what I mean? Kind of a collage, much more touch-screen, much more app for the iPad. If I had time, I'd make it.'

It doesn't need to be anything extreme, involving a 'red room' or tools and candle wax. People can source their fetishes easily via Google in less than a second, but normcore amateur porn for women is seemingly harder to find. In the current porno climate, it's clear that even something like *Fifty Shades of Grey* will do. At least it was written from a female perspective. We are so starved of sexual content written for women by women that millions went to see the cinema to see Jamie Dornan spank someone and give them an iPad in return. We're not asking for much, here.

In work, too, I found myself brainstorming about porn. I worked for an online magazine called *The Debrief* with a big sex section in it, so it was hard to avoid. I found myself being a Porn Hub regular, as I'd download their monthly reports to find out which videos were the most popular, discovering what was 'trending' each month (mainly celebrity parody videos). So yes, I really was watching porn for 'research reasons'.

Every week, the editorial team would gather round and contribute idea for articles. Our site featured a lot of risky sex content that only popped up after 6 p.m. – real talk about dildos, sex dreams, fantasies, STIs, or very niche things like what it's like to have sex on MDMA. My boss would sit us down for a 'sex brainstorm' to discuss our forthcoming features. A few times this was hosted in the middle of a pub, which was always awkward especially as in some instances the people sitting next to us would move tables, as they were clearly just trying to have a nice pint with their family while we spoke about blowjobs and bikini waxes. We decided we should probably stick to having these meetings in the office.

'So, Emma, do you want to kick off? Any ideas?' One of my senior colleagues pushed her hair back with her glasses and sat with her notepad open. Staring at me with a face that said, 'Don't you dare pitch me anything shit.'

I awkwardly shuffled my pieces of paper like an inexperienced news anchor, taking a nervous gulp and wetting my dry mouth before announcing my ideas.

'Well, firstly, I guess, I want to know if the finger-up-the-bum thing for men is a real *thing* or just an old wives' tale.' I waited for a reaction or an eye-roll. My colleagues started nodding pensively, as if it were something they wanted to know about too.

'Um, and, also some porn playlists! Or, I dunno, just a list of porn sites for twenty-something girls that aren't really creepy. You know, like … for a leisurely Sunday afternoon.'

Hearing me go forth so openly, my colleague put her hand up.

'What about how to do the sexy underwear thing, when you hate sexy underwear? I'm no Victoria's Secret model, but I'd love to wear something racy without feeling like a twat. Or, how about new sex positions that don't involve a chair? Why do all *Kama Sutra* positions involve a wooden chair?'

We then got into a heated debate about how we all felt there just wasn't anything we truly enjoyed out there, in the big World Wide Web that represented us. Not for us twenty-somethings. I turned to the intern, who looked a bit nervous.

'Do you watch porn?' I asked, casually.

'Ummmm … not really.'

'What *would* you watch though, if you had the choice? If you had the grand TV remote of all the porn in all the land?'

'Ummm … I don't know. A good-looking young couple?'

There was a pause.

'Well, maybe just girl on girl, I guess, because it feels more ethical.'

Later on, she emailed me to say she did watch it, but she just felt really embarrassed to admit it. I felt bad for putting her on the spot. I'd obviously become immune to sharing my thoughts around a table full of fellow female journalists who were shocked by nothing. It seemed that porn was something us women were taught to keep quiet about, because it's not 'polite'. If I wanted to remain polite I would not have written this chapter in my book.

*

When I broached the topic of porn with my friends, one said she felt so let down by the current Internet landscape involving porn that she'd just given up on it. Porn was actually damaging her sex life, she told me, because she'd find herself remembering some gross thing she'd seen online while she was in the middle of sex, which turned her off. She said, 'I'd rather watch a slinky sex scene in a movie than accidentally see something that turns me off.'

I agreed and told her we should think of some things we'd rather watch than what was available in the current porn climate. We made a list: the sex scene in *Black Swan*. Clive Owen entering the strip club in *Closer*. *Magic Mike*, obviously, any of the dance scenes. *Magic Mike XXL*. Any steamy scene between Mila Kunis and Zoe Saldana in *After Sex*. A freeze-frame of Johnny Depp in *Chocolat* (that lovely ponytail). The pool scene in *Wild Things*. The breathy sex scene between Reese Witherspoon and Ryan Phillippe in *Cruel Intentions* (although deeply unrealistic). The library scene in *Atonement* with James McAvoy and Keira Knightley in *that* green dress. Anything involving Idris Elba (maybe not *Mandela* though). The final scene of *In the Realm of the Senses*. Any scene from *Blue is the Warmest Colour*. That iconic *Forty Days and Forty Nights* orgasm scene with retro heart-throb Josh Hartnett. The totally unrealistic scene in *Shame* where Michael Fassbender has doggy-style sex with a woman against a glass wall in a very tall hotel building. A few bits in the James Bond films, such as the shower sex scene in one of the recent Daniel Craig films (we had different opinions on which Bond we preferred, which was to be expected). We could have gone on.

Back in university, during the film studies part of my degree, we looked at the films of Michael Winterbottom. Our course tutor referenced one called *Nine Songs*, in which the two character leads have real-life sex on screen, as well as a real ejaculation scene. Derek Malcolm from the *Guardian* said something interesting: '*Nine Songs* looks like a porn movie, but it feels like a love story.' I watched this film on repeat – so intrigued by the couple's story, romance, sex life. The critical reception was mixed, and one of the scenes became slightly iconic, as it was the first film to feature a 'footjob'. But the thing about this film was the gradual build-up to the sex scenes. When I discussed it with my friends, they admitted to enjoying the 'slow build-up' more than seeing any actual penetration on screen.

Films, we concluded, could often be sexier than porn, to women at least. (Although some movies are very much guilty of making it look like women have an orgasm in five minutes flat, *When-Harry-Met-Sally*-Herbal-Essences style. Just like in porn.) I'm not saying movies are any better or more realistic (hey, they're still *acting* – and sometimes badly), I'm just saying the actors often look like they are enjoying it more and there is something about the experience of watching a story develop in a film that can capture the imagination more. When I came out of the cinema after seeing *Magic Mike*, I went straight to the bathroom with my best friend Polly and we heard a variety of comments from lots of different-aged women: 'Oof! I need to go and sort myself out', 'How do I get my husband to do that?' and 'Get me home quickly so I can get myself off while it's all still fresh in my head!' In short: everyone was *absolutely loving it*.

2011

I found my friend Sara slumped over a hardened dish of pesto pasta that had gone cold. Her face was millimetres away from being right in it. Our other friend Jamie, Sara's housemate, had let me in, after days of my phone calls being ignored. I was starting to get increasingly worried so I had invited myself round to their north London flat. I knew something was up because I'd also heard from a friend that the previous weekend she'd binged on drugs and had ended up getting into a fight with someone in the pub. This was very unlike Sara, who was normally found in a pair of lavender-scented pyjamas watching a Richard Curtis film with a packet of Maltesers. She was my go-to advice guru. Always upbeat, always wise, always there.

It was obvious from the fact she'd been pushing me away that something wasn't right. She had been having ups and downs with her boyfriend Otis for a while, but she'd always kept herself together physically until now. We (her friends) would never have admitted it to her openly but we knew he was bad news. Now she was wearing some jogging bottoms that had dried-up cornflakes crusted into the fabric, and a top with one boob hanging out the side, and her face was down into her folded arms on the kitchen table. I hadn't seen her like this before. She had at least managed to apply her signature cat-flick eyeliner, but she still looked broken. I placed my hand on her arm and she flinched. She hadn't even noticed me come in.

'Oh, hi Emma,' she sniffled and turned towards me, hugging my middle as I stood next to her, looking and feeling helpless.

'What's happened?' I didn't know how else to ask.

Had they broken up? Had he cheated? Had someone *died*? Was she pregnant? An STI? Fired from work? Caught up in a viral video? My mind went through the list of possibilities for a twenty-something woman.

'Oh God, I can't bear to talk about it again. Jamie, can't you just tell Emma for me?'

'Come on, you can tell me,' I said, gently, rubbing her back. 'I haven't seen you for ages, come sit with me on the sofa.'

She blew into a tissue. Her nose looked sore. Her eyes bloodshot.

'Well, you know we went on a city break to Venice last week? It was meant to be beautiful … it *was* beautiful …'

'I saw your Instagram photos! Looked amazing.'

She snorted. 'Well, you clearly can't tell anything from Instagram.'

She had a point there.

'Sorry,' she continued and put the snotty tissue in her lap. 'I'm in such a terrible mood. The photos looked great. Oh, but it was shit. It all went to shit.'

She trailed off and reached for another tissue. 'He's ruined it. He's ruined everything.'

I waited for her to wipe the ball of snot away from her nose again and continue with the story. Jamie brought us over a cup of tea before tiptoeing out of the room quietly and shutting the door behind him, leaving us alone to talk.

'So you were in Venice …' I prompted her again, handing her the tea.

She inhaled. 'Yes. I went out to get some food for us in the afternoon last Sunday as we decided to have dinner in our Airbnb flat instead of going out again for food. I thought it would be really romantic. When I came back, I overheard him making strange noises in the toilet; I leaned my head against the door and I heard moaning. I thought he was in there with a girl, I mean I couldn't wrap my head around it. I had no idea what these noises were. It totally freaked me out.'

She gathered a few more breaths, trying hard not to burst into tears again.

'But then I could see through the gap in the door; he hadn't shut it properly. He was in there watching porn. Some really horrible stuff.'

I didn't know what to say. I didn't really know what this meant.

'I felt just as upset as if it were an actual real girl in there with him, do you know what I mean?'

We then did what we do best, and the perfect remedy to a difficult situation: we drank a lot of wine and asked a lot of questions. The conversation was a brutally honest one. The truth would come out after a few drinks. We soon starting slurring and ranting.

'The thing is, Em, I don't mind porn. I mean, I like the idea of it, I just hate what's offered. The girls look like they hate it, it's like a really tragically bad school play plus the most oily arses I've ever seen.'

'Did you tell him afterwards you'd seen him in the bathroom with … the porn?'

'No, I just made some noise with the pans in the kitchen so he could hear I was home, and he came out acting all normal. But do you know what really upset me? It was the fact he wasn't being affectionate with me afterwards, and didn't hint at wanting to have sex with me that night. It was our anniversary. It was like he'd got his fix from elsewhere. Well, I guess he had.'

Sara explained that the main thing, on a base level, was that she felt left out. Like he was sneaking around. The fact of the matter was: he was engaging in something sexual that didn't involve her. He was doing a thing without her, which encroached on their space, encroached on their sex life.

We had to establish that *this wasn't her fault*. Sara had started to feel awful about her own body. She had started to believe that Otis had to go online to get his kick out of porn-star women because her body was 'too normal'. I wouldn't let her compare herself to the land of silicone porn-stars. It wasn't going to be helpful for her to start contrasting herself with something staged on the screen.

Otis was picking fake five-minute clips of sexuality over the real deal and Sara was unsure as to how this could rectify itself. After they had got back from Venice she brought it up with him. He was defensive at first and then admitted he wanted to try 'other things', so they decided to break up.

I couldn't help but wonder if porn *was* the problem in all this – the access to sexual stimulants on his laptop that made him totally ignore his girlfriend who was right there in front of him.

I also couldn't help but think that this was an example of an #InternetProblem. Would Otis have avoided real-life sex in favour of printed magazines? Probably not. Even if he'd had a little look through *FHM* before Sara had come home, surely he wouldn't have had the same sort of fix? Or even an old-fashioned tits-and-bum porn magazine? The reality was, he wasn't getting off on her any more and this is what he told her. He'd become addicted to niche role-play videos and their vanilla sex wasn't cutting it. It reminded me of something John Mayer famously said in a *Playboy* interview: 'Internet pornography has absolutely changed my generation's expectations. How does that not affect the psychology of having a relationship with somebody? It's got to.' Even *Playboy* magazine itself has cut out nudity to try to target wider audiences. In a recent interview, *Playboy* CEO Scott Flanders explained why they'd made the editorial change: 'You're now one click away from every sex act imaginable for free.'

Over dinner recently, I asked a group of guy friends their thoughts on porn.

'Porn is like … an action film or something. Of course we don't think it's real. It's just entertaining. Just like with *Grand Theft Auto*, we'd never steal a car and run someone over in real life … it's the same with porn – we don't expect to do the things we see on the screen.'

I found this comment on porn interesting – and again it made me think the porn industry is missing an emotional layer. It's visually stimulating and exciting like an action movie – but what about the softer narratives? What about the gentler storylines that aren't over-the-top spectacles?

The idea that an addiction to on-screen content is pushing away our real-life experiences is an interesting one. Not only in association with porn. It made me wonder what else we might substitute in real life for its Internet equivalent. Is it making us lazier? Or just spoilt for choice? Online food ordering, online dating, online livestreaming gigs, shows and events without leaving the house. An alternate virtual reality. Potentially we're still in a phase where our Internet addiction is taking over more of our lives than it should because we don't yet have the tools to curb it. Like little kids who don't have a bedtime, we're constantly logging onto a Wifi connection, not knowing when it's time to stop.

Addiction to any sort of online behaviour is easy. Porn addicts. Gaming addicts. Social media addicts (I am one). I question whether to call it an addiction, yet I find myself running home to charge my phone, getting visibly panicked when I'm on my last percentage of battery and standing by a plug socket while my phone charges. Having 1 per cent of battery left is something I could dress up as for Halloween. I check Twitter too many times a day to admit. Refreshing pages. Ctrl + R. I get aggressive when the hotel Wifi doesn't work.

I'm now at an age where I know what I want to Google and what I don't want to Google. I have barriers and I know what to block and mute from my social media feeds. Therefore I feel more in control of what I discover. But if I'd had a smartphone or laptop during my early teen years, God knows what I would have searched for. I don't know what I would have seen or stumbled upon. Young kids have iPads and they have search engines at their fingertips. I just hope that what they see online, especially in the porn world, doesn't affect their real-life relationships. I hope that by the time the next generation grows up, they start seeing elements of real life reflected back at them instead of fake sexuality.

'Unhealthy Life Choices Barbie comes with a BA in English, an unfinished manuscript, a fifth of vodka and a Twitter account.'

@LaurenDeStefan

chapter 8
Getting an Internet Job

2010

Here are five reasons I think I accidentally ended up in a career in social media:

1. When I was six I used to spend hours typing on my nan's old typewriter despite the fact all the vowel keys were missing and there was no paper inserted. I just liked pressing the buttons, okay?

2. I won 'Most Obsessed with Myspace' in my 2007 School Yearbook, and I wasn't even embarrassed.

3. I love connection and conversation: I moved schools three times between the ages of eight and eleven and learned how to make friends with just about anyone, immediately (sometimes I'd bring in random stuff from my bedroom, like hair clips or temporary press-on tattoos, and offer them to people as free gifts).

4. Despite liking making new friends, I prefer online interactions from my sofa than a booming party (apparently it's not socially acceptable to bring your laptop and a book to a party).

5. My parents are the most sociable people I know and taught me from an early age how to 'mingle', especially at their dinner parties. Twitter is the 'cocktail party' of the Internet, after all.

My first internship? Oh, let me tell you about it. First, we must gather around a campfire in hoodies, like an opening scene of *Are You Afraid of the Dark?* Like many internships, the whole set-up was slightly confusing mainly because you have to say 'thank you' to people who outwardly hate you. It is fetishised and glamourised through movies like *The Devil Wears Prada* and episodes of *The Hills*, as though it's super chic to get screeched at for getting a Starbucks order slightly wrong. I too imagined myself in a film montage to the *Rocky* theme tune sweating down Madison Avenue with big Saks bags as a cute man winked at me and hailed me a cab while high-fiving my cool boss who loved me. The reality (for me) was lugging a bag of 150 bottles of Head & Shoulders along Oxford Circus back to the office and having to shove a folded-up (clean) sanitary pad in the back of my heel to soothe a blister as I couldn't waste any time going into Boots. But hey, I felt lucky at the time to even be doing *that*.

I cannot hand on heart tell you if my internship taught me any skills apart from 1) how to actually get one without already being family friends with the bald CEO of the company; 2) how to deal with humiliation on a daily basis; 3) how to survive on one packet of dried-up noodles a week for lunch; and 4) how you should never, ever ask anything if you can Google it first.

But, I get it, this is how they sort the wheat from the chaff in the industry. *How far will you go to be totally ripped apart emotionally? Which damp floor will you sleep on to keep your 'job'? How will you repair your totally damaged ego? How will you handle making multiple cups of tea for people that treat you like you are the understudy to the person playing Oliver Twist in a really shit play? No, you cannot have any more money. Go away, and stand behind that curtain.*

After graduating from university, I was shocked to suddenly find myself back at home three years later, at the very same table that I'd sat at to apply to university, sitting in the very same chair, in the very same crusty dressing gown, with zero idea of what I wanted to be, or who I wanted to be. I desperately tried to remind myself what I did during that three years of my life, which seemed to be mostly made up of drinking beer in bed, smoking cigarettes outside the library, having sex with emotionally inept boys or spending the last of my pennies going drunk-shopping. Half of my degree was English Literature, with very stern lecturers who would stand in the front of the room with their eyes closed and recite medieval poetry from memory. The other half was a film degree with guest lectures from the likes of Mark Kermode, who I secretly fancied, which turned out to be the best incentive to actually get me to my lecture on time. A few weeks before the last-ever day of university, a slightly frazzled professor burst into our lecture theatre and told us to put down our pens. It seemed important. He was preparing us for some news, perhaps.

'I just wanted to say goodbye to everyone as I'm on holiday tomorrow. Stay strong. Out of this entire group only 20 per cent of you will get jobs straight away or in fact any job at all. And 5 per cent will actually end up liking those jobs. The rest of you: good luck. I'm sorry.' He then left the room abruptly and slammed the door. We then all plodded along in the rain to the pub.

So, of course this didn't help with my reluctance about going out into the 'real world'. I did what any nervous post-grad would do, and stared at my laptop while Googling 'LONDON JOBS' – the broadest of all Google searches – in a desperate attempt to stumble across anything. In my cover letter I described myself, cringingly, as a 'fresh graduate, with fresh ideas!' I applied for lots of things and got twelve rejection emails in less than an hour. Because, plot twist: you need *experience* in order to get work *experience. Duh.*

I heard back from someone at a PR agency in Reading (close enough to London: at this point I wasn't being picky) so I jumped in the family car and drove up there, to what seemed like the greyest building in the world. It reminded me of something out of *The Office* but without David Brent to break the ice. They made me fill out two pages of 'ideas for creative campaigns involving a new gluten-free food brand' and then I never heard back. Coincidentally, a few weeks later, I saw some of my ideas, word for word, pop up on their website in a campaign they'd successfully pitched to a small gluten-free business. That was nice of them. It was a sweet and sour feeling because even though I was still jobless and penniless (and they had ignored me *and* stolen from me), at least I now knew my ideas were pretty darn good. Maybe I'd be good at something, I thought. Idea theft already!

Then came more rejection emails. Luckily, a job interview eventually came through. I went back up to London, and sat anxiously across from two women in grey suits, while staring hungrily at the plate of croissants on the boardroom table, unsure if the etiquette was to dive in or if they were like display pillows on hotel sofas, there to look good, but not to touch. They asked me about my financial PR experience (I had none, and ironically my personal financial experience was in dire straits) and they seemed confused when I didn't know the names of many European banks. There and then, after exchanging a few concerned looks with each other, they mentioned that I might be better suited for a more *consumer-friendly* type of job. I think in business-speak this translates as 'something fluffier'. They said I seemed 'nice enough' and they'd try to hook me up with an internship in another department of the PR agency. I could go home, have five days to research the department and the case studies and the team over there would quiz me over the phone. I paraphrased their 'About Us' section off the website in my interview and got the job.

A few weeks later, I packed my bags to live in my uncle's basement in Kent, outside London, so that I could take the Tunbridge Wells to Charing Cross train each morning at 6.30 a.m. to get to my desk on time. My uncle and his husband would look after me by cooking hearty dinners and we'd have a cigarette out of the window while I told them all about the boys I fancied at work. It was 2010, the iconic year of Cher Lloyd and One Direction as contestants on *The X Factor*. My monthly earnings were the equivalent of £11,000 a year. I had to feel lucky that I'd talked my way into the company, a global PR firm situated just off Soho Square. On walking up to the entrance I saw Guy Ritchie lock up his bike at the film studios next door and felt like I was walking in slow motion. It was totally surreal that I was in London, let alone somewhere in Soho, let alone where Guy Ritchie locks up his bike. I squealed when I saw my desk phone and computer, and when Jess, the boss's PA who sat next to me, informed me about the Friday drinks trolley and the fact we could get snacks from the downstairs bar if we just swiped our employee card. This is where I began my solitary diet of cheesy Quavers and white wine.

What I soon realised, though, was that the drinks trolley, the extravagant parties, the free moisturisers and champagne on tap was not going to pay my rent, or pay for anything in fact. I wondered, quite early on, whether these 'perks' were the company's cover-up mechanism for not paying anyone very much. It seemed the free shampoo from clients was distracting people from complaining about the fact they weren't being paid in actual pound coins. I noticed this at other firms I worked at too: when that time of year came round and they announced they couldn't give anyone bonuses, they'd throw a huge party instead to divert everyone. I'd go along to the grand ball, usually masquerade-themed, and spend most of the evening moaning that the gold-encrusted cupcakes were nice, but I'd rather they'd given me the cash instead. Great for Instagram, not so great for my back pocket.

What I didn't mind, however, was being the office dogsbody, which was to be expected. Everyone around me was very stressed with their Very Important Action Lists and I was just revelling in the fact that I had a proper desk space that was all mine. I would call my best friend daily:

'Hello, only me!'

'Hi, what's up?'

'Oh, nothing, I'm just calling you from my *work phone*, because I'm at *work*.'

My intern 'jobs' were wide and varied, and included:

1. Being dressed up in wires and cables as a sort of mascot
This was a strange one. One day an email landed in my inbox.

'Hi Emma, please can you go to Maplin on Great Portland Street and grab some big chunky cables and any wires, quite thick ones if possible. Just ask someone in there for help – they're just for props so you don't need to be picky. Can you have this done by the time I'm back from my manicure?'

Wondering what they were needed for, I went on my merry way with the company card and purchased lots of different-sized cables as briefed. I was part of a team working on a campaign for a new wireless gadget. The campaign video was a parody of a horror movie with big Tangled Wire Monsters. The idea behind the video concept was basically: don't let your loose wires or cables get tangled up because they will come and eat you in the middle of the night. I soon realised that these weird marketing campaigns were always based on fear. If you didn't want to be eaten by a wire monster, you could buy this wireless gizmo for £80!

I know what you're thinking: it sounds *just* like *Mad Men*. So for the 'media drops' (where you take the product to the press and try to 'sell it in' to them) my manager asked me to go to companies such as Universal, Myspace and Red Bull Media House. Some of the biggest media names in London. And the reason I'd been asked to buy all these wires is because someone thought it would be a good idea if I turned up at the door of these huge companies as the Tangled Wire Monster mascot. I found myself agreeing to it (I was constantly worried I'd get fired and be back in my dressing gown at home) so three helpers started Sellotaping them to my body and tying them around my neck. I had about twenty-five different wire cables hanging off me. I'm sure I don't need to tell you that when I arrived at these huge important buildings anyone who came into contact with me was a) very confused and b) felt incredibly sorry for me. I arrived at the Myspace headquarters and a senior director there just looked at me blankly and said: 'What the fuck?'

2. Building ten huge toy boxes from scratch, using one broken Allen key

One idea for a washing detergent campaign was to send large toy boxes to top-tier 'mummy bloggers' and get some of them personalised with their child's name on. It was my job to source the toy boxes from the Internet, get them delivered and, to my delight, BUILD THEM in the post room using nothing but a dodgy Allen key, before sending them out to the recipients. One night my colleague Nadia found me sweatily weeping into a big toy box, with a thumb covered in blood, pulling out splinters and sobbing at the turn my rubbish life had taken. It seems I'd worked so hard for a degree only to be employed to build wooden objects alone in a dark basement with two weak wrists and no clue about how to use a power drill.

3. Getting thirty drunk bald men into taxis at 2 a.m. (in priority order)

Getting rich, drunk, bald men into taxis after a boozy client event sounds doable, if only the task were that simple. But I had to make sure the most important went first. This was especially hellish as ironically the least important businessmen had the biggest egos and shouted at me when their taxi was delayed. In addition, they all shared the same toffy names. I had to tick each one off the list, while they yelled at me for not sorting them out first or slurred something about my legs. Each man was the most important person at the party in his eyes so I had to simultaneously manage my clipboard list and massage their egos. My boss pulled me aside later, a few minutes after the storm.

'I saw the chaos.' She lowered her voice. 'Really ... well done.'

Things started to change slightly when I was allowed to do some *actual* PR work, which consisted of ringing a list of journalists and hoping and praying that they would miraculously be interested in the wireless gadget we were endlessly trying to plug. My luck hit the jackpot when a senior editor from a tabloid paper wanted to meet for lunch because he was doing a feature on wireless technology, so I took my boss's American Express, booked us into the Dean Street Townhouse and anxiously waited for him to arrive. A man with thin grey hair came straight over to me, introduced himself and ordered a huge glass of red wine. I stuck with a Diet Coke. Later I watched him guzzle down the most expensive dish on the menu while I awkwardly tried to explain how the gadget worked. Of course it was being temperamental and not working the way it should be. He just nodded along, in between mouthfuls. It was all rather excruciating. I didn't have much hope of anything coming from our meeting.

A few days later, I arrived at my desk and my colleagues were eerily quiet. I had just sat down and logged into my computer when I heard my boss's swivel chair turn on its wheels.

'Emma!'

I saw on her screen she'd just run a report, as she did each morning, to check what coverage we'd had. Normally it was dodgy tech websites that no one really read and would later shut down, or 'gadget bloggers' who had about fifteen loyal readers, the types of geeks who would probably get boners from a limited-edition plug socket. But now she was waving a newspaper and showing her teeth. I think she was smiling.

'You managed to get the product in Celebrity X's *New!* magazine column. WELL DONE YOU! He loved it!'

When I realised this might one day be my 'career highlight' I felt slightly sick to the stomach. I'd successfully got a B-list celebrity to mention our client's battery brand.

She then slammed down a copy of the tabloid paper on my desk, the same tabloid that the senior editor I'd taken for lunch worked at, which featured a full page dedicated to the wireless gadget. She beamed at me, which she'd never done before.

'You. Well fucking done.'

My boss was the swearing type. When I did something good she'd shout in my face and curse at me and I had to learn that this was a *good* thing. Her shouting: 'You motherfucker!' did not mean she hated me or was about to fire me, but quite the opposite.

After that point, I had pressure on me to beat this coverage. I was told my job was to get another celebrity to try and use the gadget. I was given a log-in to a secret database that held the names and phone numbers of celebrities. I rang one well-known TV presenter and he told me he was on holiday (whoops) with his family (double whoops) and was extremely pissed off, and 'How the fuck did I get this mobile number?' It was a good question. I decided not to further upset him by saying it happened to be on a database that every single publicist in the world could access.

Every time I rang someone I got a response that was a variation on the theme of 'eff off'. I didn't blame them. As soon as I started to realise my job was going to be hounding people and secretly finding out people's personal mobile phone numbers, I started to go off it. I would flashback to being an awkward twelve-year-old, phoning people who politely (and often not so politely) told me they didn't want to hang out with me.

The next instalment of the campaign was to contact a list of bloggers. This was five years ago, so at this point it really meant nothing to me. A blogger? A what now? We started to contact bloggers to write about things and send them free products, hoping for a review. Embroidered dressing gowns with their initials on, or big make-up kits, or free towels.

I knew instantly that blogging was something I wanted to do myself – I certainly did not want to continue contacting Z-list celebrities. What would be the worst thing that could happen if I bought my own domain name and started to put stuff I enjoyed on my own blog? These bloggers were in control of their own *thing*. And the prospect of getting a few free towels couldn't hurt either.

One of the company directors approached me one evening (we were still in the office at 10 p.m.) and asked if I could come with her to the glass meeting room by the kitchen. Naturally, I thought I was in trouble. In fact, every single time anyone said my name I thought it would be followed by a public firing. I did steal some notepads from the stationery cupboard to take home and write ideas for blog posts earlier that week. Maybe they'd seen. I was paranoid they'd fire me for starting a blog.

'Hi, Em. Sorry to disturb you, I know it's late. But I wondered if you could teach me how to use all those digital tools you use? How you get all of those statistics from the brand conversations happening on Twitter, Facebook and stuff, and how to do those graphs showing our engagement levels? Oh and WordPress, can you teach me WordPress and HTML? Like tonight?'

I said that was fine but it might have to be the next day because I had to finish all the work she'd given me to do before then.

'Oh God, of course! Finish all the stuff I gave you first. It's just that I'm actually leaving the company to go elsewhere in a few weeks, and all that social media digital stuff will really come in handy. They are paying me loads of money to know all this stuff but, if I'm *honest*, I don't have a clue.' She snorted.

At this point it dawned on me that although I was absolutely appalling at handling spreadsheets, I actually knew quite a bit about the Internet and specifically how to market and build things online. And this knowledge was *valuable*. I decided there and then that something needed to change. Essentially, I needed to grow a pair and ask to be paid some actual money. It was the calm before the social media storm; brands were experimenting with launching their own Facebook pages for the first time and I felt that this was about to all take off.

I knew I had more to offer the company: after all, if one of the company directors wanted to pick *my* brain I knew there was an opportunity here. Why was I so scared of not being liked? I suddenly had a flash-forward and imagined myself chained to this desk in five years' time, all because I wasn't brave enough to have the conversation that *I was better than putting bald businessmen into taxis*. I didn't want anyone thinking I was rude or arrogant. But I had I knew I had a brain, and it was all too easy to be a girl in a company not asking for what she wanted. I'd once got chatting to a female colleague in the kitchen while we both made tea and she told me she wanted to leave. When I asked her why she hadn't, she said, 'Oh, you know. I don't want them to get annoyed, or think I'm cheeky.' I noticed that the men didn't seem to care if they were disliked, storming around the building like they owned the place (maybe because they probably did *actually* own the building), but the women I met were too afraid to ask for more money out of fear of looking 'impolite'. The men in my life told me to go where the money is.

Whenever I rang my dad I got the same response: 'Money, Emma! Ask for more money.'

'How?' I'd ask.

'You go in there, and then you ask. Say: "I'd like more money."'

He was being lovely and helpful as always, but I could also tell he was confused by the fact I didn't seem to understand how simple this was.

So I went to see one of our directors for a chat. I was promptly told I was lucky to be there. I told them I couldn't afford to top up my travel card *to even get into work*. My boss said she could up my pay ever so slightly (we're talking a few more quid a month) but there was nothing drastic she could do as it wouldn't be fair on the other juniors in the office. If Sheryl Sandberg had been around on my book shelf at this point, she would have told me to Lean In. I tried leaning in and asking for more, but it didn't work, so I leaned out and quit the job – and I'm so glad I did. Quitting can actually turn out quite well, so it seems, especially when you can ask another company for more money. This was my first foray into growing a thicker skin, making new opportunities and getting closer to what I wanted in the workplace.

It was clear my heart was in the digital world. I had a blog; I spent my days on Twitter looking for like-minded geeks. I didn't want to sell in stories about battery brands to print newspapers forever. There was also something in the air: social media started becoming a talking point among huge corporate brands and their parent companies. So in 2010, I started going to free 'social media' events hosted on Brick Lane such as Twestival (yes, you guessed, a Twitter festival) and I met a guy called Matt who introduced me to a few people. Matt was really smart. When it came to technology, new app launches or platforms that made life easier, he was the one who knew everything before it was 'a thing'.

I wanted to be in this newfound social media scene, where everyone wore a beanie and knew how to 'analyse metrics of success'. They knew digital shortcuts to everything and companies were paying them heaps of money to do cool stuff with their brands in the digital space. It was 2010, and they were already selling in augmented reality to some of the biggest brands in the world. I wanted in with this new geeky crowd who were beta-testing new apps over their pints. I made a friend called Julie, who would update me on the latest plugins for WordPress and gave me a book called *Marketing in the Groundswell* by Charlene Li and Josh Bernoff, a book that without me knowing at the time would sum up my future career.

If you work in social media, you have to be up to date on the newest tools and innovations every single day. Every day. The tables turned, with the youngest people in the company feeling more confident with the new launches. I remember it even now, more senior employees shouting across the office, 'What the fuck is a Tumblr meme?' Back in the day, to progress in your career you would learn how to do a specific job via your older mentors and it took years and years to get promoted. Hierarchy was strong, and age equalled experience. But not in the digital world.

My first real 'Internet job' was Online Community Manager for one of the world's largest beauty brands. It was the type of job that I found difficult to explain to relatives or friends who worked in traditional employment – perhaps because I was worried about being judged. Essentially, I looked after a global Facebook page – a page that worked closely with Facebook HQ itself and one that had grown from 2 million to 13 million fans in a year. There were executives from fifty different countries all posting their content to the one page. Behind the scenes, I would speak to the Community Managers in each country, working with them on the 'best practice' of the content (i.e. status updates and images) that they had to post. Although it seemed totally nuts that it was such a military operation to run a Facebook page for a big brand, it really was amazing to speak to people in so many countries all around the world. I felt like I was truly connecting with their cultures in a different way.

Whenever people would say, 'So you literally just post stuff on Facebook for a living?' I wanted to explain the complexity of working for a global brand, the layers of communication, the fact that I was learning how to market via social media before it exploded, how a brand could communicate consistently in many different countries, and how to get messages across in a new and exciting way. No day was the same – the world and the platforms we used constantly changed, and if you weren't ahead of the game, you were left very far behind.

Jobs like this didn't exist even six years ago, so it was impossible to get any hand-me-down rule books or successor tips, it was just hard and fast and totally changeable each day. I learned from the smart people around me, but I also used my initiative to pitch proactively. If I took my eyes off the ball even for a moment, I'd be behind, the idiot in the meeting room. On our Skype group, thousands of links would be shared every day about new technological advances – updates to Google, for example – and you were expected to read them all and digest every article. Trends were constantly moving: new applications launched, old things died out, new ways of doing things emerged, new online magazines were started up, new inventions were announced. Part of the job was being the person who knew the Internet inside out, to constantly be on top of all of it. Never dropping the ball.

The good thing about learning social media marketing skills before the world and its wife started calling themselves a Social Media Guru was that I learned how to market my own work and my own writing. Magazines was where my heart truly was. As a young kid I would wander over to the magazine bit in Sainsbury's and put my nose in the glossy pages. I would wonder about the real lives of the celebrities and the people who put together the magazine. Who chose which stories to put in each issue. What the lives of these journalists were like. Magazines and editorial websites were about storytelling, whereas working for brands was storytelling but within a sales framework. Although you were still selling advertising in magazines, I felt there must be more creative freedom in a job like that than when you were writing tweets for a toothpaste brand.

I made a zigzag move by building up my own portfolio of free content on my blog but also on websites such as the *Huffington Post*'s blogger network. It seemed the right thing to do at the time but now I'm into a paid writing career I have mixed feelings about having written so much for *Huffington Post*. On the one hand, it was great exposure for my writing right at the beginning when no one was reading my blog or knew I could write. It gave me an opportunity to come up with my own topics, write about them, run them past an editor and get them posted on a huge platform. I used the *Huffington Post* name to my advantage. I emailed the people whose jobs I admired and asked if I could interview them for the blogs network. I ended up interviewing BBC Radio 1 producer, a journalist at *Elle* and even Alesha Dixon at Team GB

House during the 2012 Olympics. Often my pieces would appear on the home page, which I thought was a wonderful way of getting lots of readers of the *Huffington Post* potentially stumbling across my work and then maybe following me on Twitter. However, they didn't pay. I wrote on there for four years without them paying me a bean. I've read lots of think pieces about how unethical this is of *Huffington Post*, a huge network bought by AOL for millions. But, if I'm being totally honest, I got something out of it at the time. I was a nobody and people were reading and sharing my work. I still had a full-time job, so I was blogging for them in the evenings. I didn't feel exploited at the time – but to not pay writers in general once they are actually good at what they do? That is nonsense. My motto now is simply this: say yes to everything; then say no to everything. I swore that the minute I built my own platform and got a portfolio of work that I would never write for free again. Because, guess what: writers should get paid. It's amazing how many people will try and get away with not paying you for your words. Because 'it's competitive' and 'we can give you exposure!' Did you know: you can't buy anything in Topshop with 'exposure'?

During my lunch breaks I would log on to the journalist database I had access to so I could write down their email addresses, and from my personal account I sent out some pretty desperate 'please let me write for you!' emails. And to my utter surprise, I didn't get the big tumbleweed I was expecting, but instead got replies. Again, it was either writing for free or for peanuts but I got a weekly gig writing for the *Telegraph* whereby I curated lists of the most 'viral' stories each week for their website. Then two lucky escapes happened one after the other. I went for an interview at *Company* magazine, but I wasn't experienced enough in features writing so they gave the job to someone else. The print magazine folded a few months later. I then applied to work at another new online venture behind a big publishing house, and that folded a year later too.

That's when I got my first job as Social Media Editor for a magazine. It means taking content from a website, and selling it across social media in an interesting way. It's growth strategy, it's content creation, it's customer service, it's a branding exercise. It also means hosting things like Twitter Q&As with celebrities. Instead of an old-school interview, tools like Twitter are amazing for exploring a celebrity's personality in a more informal way, responding to 140-character tweets. I've been in the same room as Kate Winslet, Amy Schumer, Drew Barrymore, Toni Collette and Rebel Wilson, live-tweeting their responses. A job in social media can be nuts.

My family and friends don't always understand what I do. And that's because not only do I have a weird job title, I also have more than one job. We truly are Generation Slashie – meaning our job titles are starting to allow more 'slashes' to them. Having one job is starting to become rarer. You might be a director-slash-dentist. Or blogger-slash-journalist. Or doctor-slash-painter. Now that we live in a world of social profiles and snappy bios, we are not defined just by our nine-to-five any more. We are free to choose to define ourselves by our creative outlet, our desk job, our hobbies, our lifestyle or a random project we are currently working on. And I like it.

In 2016, social media jobs have gone through the roof, with 70 per cent of marketers saying they will increase their social media spend across the board. A search on LinkedIn reveals that over 55,000 people have the word 'influencer' in their titles. Companies are getting more 'hip' and modern and undergoing massive structural re-shuffles, plus introducing new roles. People are now not just account managers but 'writers', 'curators', 'chief brainstormers' or niche specialists, such as 'head of LGBTQ content' for example. I often go searching on LinkedIn just to come across new job titles, as it's so interesting. I was never told at school or university to stand out from the crowd and turn my most distinguishing features into a job; I was told to do what everyone else was doing and go on a traditional graduate scheme. I thought everything was a bit old-fashioned in my first graduate job ('You want me to SCAN this? You what?') – turns out everything just takes a while to adapt to change. Finally, the more forward-thinking companies realised it's actually much cleverer these days to take risks before their competitors do. My favourite memories of working life have been those times when I've got my strait-laced employers to take a risk on something that sometimes failed, sometimes wildly succeeded. Routines won't save you when it comes to the Internet. The Internet is the ultimate boss, and will make or break you, depending on what mood it's in.

We're in a weird and exciting media moment, where things launch and fold as quickly as each other. We're having to re-train ourselves almost daily on new platforms, new formats, new delivery of things. Funny GIFs with spot-on captions. Breaking old habits, learning new ones. Re-learning what people want, how they want it, when they want it. I don't think us millennials care as much about working for a 'big brand' any more. Given the choice, would you choose a 'known' brand over a newer venture? Does a traditional paper really have more clout than a new Internet platform any more? Is it a generational thing? Start-ups have become way sexier to work for than a household name our grandparents would recognise. The cool kids set up camp at their kitchen table and that's where the magic happens. Just wait: soon we'll all be freelancers.

'You don't have a career. You have a life. Do the work.'

Cheryl Strayed

chapter 9
Just Another WordPress Blog

2011

'Emma. Do you have five minutes?'

I looked up from my desk, hoping my new boss's boss didn't just see that I was actually on Pinterest, looking for some house-plant inspiration.

'I want you to go and do a talk at an awards ceremony in a few days. It's about blogging. People are interested in blogs. You have one, don't you?'

My boss's boss was a big cheese in the media industry – the managing director of the digital team of a global PR agency I worked at. He was an American who knew all the best restau-rants and expensive cocktail places in London and was always mingling with other important CEOs, always in and out of secret meetings with Facebook or Google. I'd send him a link to a new app or platform update and he'd nod over his coffee and say, 'Ah, yes I've been playing with the beta version of this for a while.' He wore a large blazer and quirky glasses, and he was as friendly down the pub as he was in the office, genuinely interested in what you were doing with your life. When I first met him we were in a local pub next to our office and I assumed he was a colleague's dad. He was totally down to earth, despite his power and importance within the industry, and I really respected his opinion on things – not because he was a man but because he took the time to notice everyone's individual habits and talents.

He'd picked up on the fact that I was into blogging on the side of my job and it meant a lot to me that it was being taken seriously. Most employers would wrinkle their nose if they found out one of their employees had side-projects. Instead of thinking it must be because I wasn't working hard enough, he'd understood that it must mean I was working *harder* somehow to fit it all in. Bosses who didn't agree with me being creative in my own time really affected me but then the decision would become clear: I shouldn't be working for them. Companies that kill creativity are rife, and I wasn't prepared to kill the things I loved to fit into a box just like everybody else.

But this boss was different: he'd notice an employee's passion for something and make sure he threw that person into it further. He soon got me writing for the company blog and had me connecting with like-minded people in our other offices: 'You should really get talking to Amy in the LA office – she has a blog too, you two would get on.' He'd open doors for me, introduce me to people and make me feel like I could achieve exciting things if I kept putting the hard work in. He would also be the one person who firmly injected fun into the grey-suited office environment. When things got a bit stale he would come barrelling in from the South by Southwest festival and report back on the latest trends, getting everyone fired up and excited about the latest virtual reality headset or longform storytelling app. His brain would vibrate at a slightly different frequency. He was ahead of the game. Bored with what everyone else thought was 'innovative' because that would already mean it was behind the times. He was always chasing the next big thing for his clients, and his team.

'An awards ceremony sounds fun! When?' I asked, trying not to sound too nervous.

'In a few days. It will be fun, don't worry about it.' He could clearly see the dread on my face. 'Oh and by the way, it's in Turkey. We're just booking the flights to Istanbul for you. You'll need to do a thirty-minute talk on personal branding and blogging for the Turkish Blog Awards.'

I mean, I couldn't say no. But my stomach did a flip.

When I arrived in Turkey the following week, I travelled to my hotel room and got myself ready, while a taxi waited outside to take me straight to the conference building. Once there, I had to stand in front of a branded board advertising the awards and have my photo taken, and do a five-minute talk to camera about the future of the blogging industry. I have never felt so on the spot, having to say something that *sort of* made sense which would then go live on a website a few minutes later. I peered into the room and there were over 200 seats. My stomach niggled away at me. What did I know about blogging? My blog was still fairly new. Everywhere I looked, there were huge cameras recording me and famous Turkish radio presenters ready to stick a microphone in my face. I felt like an imposter. Little did I know, this wouldn't be the first time in my career that'd I feel this way. The dreaded imposter syndrome had started creeping in. In the moments I should be feeling successful, I was feeling anxious instead.

On the stage, all my words were being translated into Turkish, and the questions coming in from the moderator were translated into my ear. I was on a panel with three middle-aged business-men and I didn't get much air time, but I tried not to think that this was because I was a blonde twenty-two-year-old in a fuschia Topshop dress sandwiched between men in crisp suits. I refused not to be taken seriously and sat up straight in my seat, pretend-ing to be confident. This was a lesson I'd learn over and over again: pretending to be confident slowly but surely turns into real confidence.

During the Q&A, someone asked one of the men on the panel if he 'felt famous' because he had 6,000 Twitter followers. He replied that yes, he did, a bit. I smirked at a woman in the audience who I thought had rolled her eyes with me, but no one else did. They just had their pens out and were scribbling everything down. Six thousand Twitter followers was apparently a big deal. Clearly this was the start of the numbers fame game.

The next question that came in from the audience was directed straight to me. I paused as the words got translated into English into my ear.

Hello, Emma. I work in advertising here in Istanbul. Do you run ads on your blog? And what ad units do you run, and how?

I knew that most people were starting to run advertising on their blogs, but I was only two years into launching mine so I didn't know too much about it. I just thought I was there to talk about writing fun articles and how to grow an audience. I suddenly realised why they had wanted me to attend: they wanted to find out about monetisation. They were hungry for answers.

The microphone was thrust into my face while I stuttered over my words. As soon as I finished, another question came straight in.

Tell us how to make money from blogs.

'Currently, I don't advertise on the side bars on my blogs, but I know many that do. I do partner with brands for sponsored blog posts, because they don't differ hugely from my natural editorial pieces, and I'm really clear when I've been sent a few free items of clothes, or vouchers, or money.'

Why don't you do affiliate marketing?

'I might in the future,' I said. 'But for now I just use my blog to write and connect with other people.' There was a general murmur in the crowd, as if to say: why doesn't she advertise? I felt like I'd let the crowd down; I got the impression they wanted to hear from someone who made big bucks from their blog. But it just wasn't why I was blogging. I was doing it to just share my writing with the world. And everyone in the audience look confused when I kept saying that.

How much money do you make?

I paused for a moment, and felt that in any other situation being asked your salary in front of an audience of 200 people would be considered rude. I managed to sidestep the question by saying that it varied. Because it did. I hadn't been ready to start commercialising my own blog because I was petrified of losing my authentic writer's voice. Plus I didn't know enough about it yet.

Would you work with a brand that you didn't like if they offered you a lot of money?

I don't know if this question was an attempt to trip me up or they were just genuinely curious, but I thought the answer was quite obvious. In the right situations, having brand sponsors can be a wonderful and mutually beneficial experience. But it's clear that if something's not right, you turn it down. My fellow YouTuber friends turn down a hell of a lot of opportunities not to break the bond with their fans. One friend specifically turned down the chance to be sponsored by a Hollywood movie because it didn't feel right. They get so much cynicism about the fact they are making good money but you don't see half of the stuff they also say no to in order to stay true to themselves. For people who only do things for money, this is not really something they can wrap their head around. But in a creative line of work, you make sacrifices to believe in what you're doing.

I grabbed the microphone: 'If you love your blog, you will not damage its reputation or kill it with adverts that disrupt the content. An honest blog is the only way it can be successful, in my opinion.'

So in the cases that you do work with brands, how can you sponsor your words, if you consider yourself a writer?

This is where I got stuck, because I didn't have the answer. I mumbled something about the need to make sure that the brand totally understood my blog and my writing style, and that anything they were offering could seamlessly make a really interesting blog post. Sometimes the content really doesn't have to be all about the product or company. It's more likely that users will engage with it if it's not heavily branded. I didn't know what it meant at the time, but I had begun talking about native advertising.

I went back to my hotel that night freaked out at the thought of monetising the one thing that had brought me so much joy. How can you monetise the words that you really feel so deeply they almost vibrate out of you? It was something I'd have to work out privately, because I knew my blog was different to the fashion and beauty blogs. It's easy to wear a particular nail varnish or talk about a brand's new SS16 collection without it looking forced. It's easy to wear sponsored clothes if all you love writing about is fashion. But I'd have to be careful not to lose readers. Anything that wasn't clearly my 'vibe' would stick out like a sore thumb. A recent article on *Globe and Mail* stated that American blogger Tavi Gevinson rejects working with certain brands, such as anti-ageing creams, because her site is for teenagers. This is what I'm talking about!

Would you read a novel by your new favourite author if you found out they had a sponsorship deal with Coca-Cola? Would it be weird if Hermione in the final Harry Potter novel was always using Carmex lip balm because of money exchanged behind the scenes? Would you enjoy sending your mates emojis if they were sponsored by particular food brands? How far do we want to go with interweaving selling stuff into our real, authentic lives? How would you feel if your favourite people didn't disclose that they were sponsored?

That evening, after the awards wrapped up, there was a big party for all the Turkish media and other European magazines. I ended up drinking Efes beers with a journalist from the Dutch *Telegraaf* and the chief designer from German website bilde.de (Germany's answer to the *Sun*) at a bar looking out onto the Bosphorus, with people smoking and dancing all around me. The world seemed very small all of a sudden, and everyone wasn't exactly sure what the 'future of blogs' would be, but I was meeting people in the media industry and I was very, very, very excited by it all.

When I created my new WordPress blog in 2009, the 'place-holder' before you inputted your own blog title said: 'Just Another

WordPress Blog'. And that's exactly what it was. It was just another blog, among the millions of others. I had created Just Another Blog that would probably never get discovered. Even though that was a depressing truth, the exciting thing was that it was all mine: one person might read it, or 10,000 people, or no one. I didn't care. I wanted an online diary, and an online diary is exactly what I created. If I were to give Virginia Woolf's quote a little millennial update I'd say 'a woman must have money and an online space of her own'.

When I started my blog, I didn't realise that writing short pieces on my own makeshift website would lead me to discovering more about myself than ever before, while also leading me directly to my dream career. By doing what I loved with no agenda and no expectations, I was unwittingly guiding myself towards something I didn't even know existed in the far-away grown-up distance. I didn't realise at the time how a blog could connect you to so many people – and that by displaying your most vulnerable thoughts online, you could make some surprising and brilliant friendships.

The reason my blog makes me so happy, when it really comes down to it, is the freedom it brings me. Human beings fundamentally like to be heard, understood and connected with others. The Internet has offered this. I've had times when I've felt totally suffocated in real life, be it down to the house I was living in, the people around me, relationship problems or a job I hated. But whatever happens, however bad real life gets, I can always mentally escape on my blog, even if I can't physically. Diving into my blog often feels like the bit in *Mary Poppins* where Bert and the kids all jump into the street painting, holding umbrellas in the rain and spending the whole day bouncing around on horse carousels, eating toffee apples and loving life.

When bloggers started out, no one really knew there was money to be made. In a world in which we were riddled with fake-looking company-sponsored testimonials of products featuring all-American blonde women reading slowly from a script, honest blogger reviews were very welcome. We could instead listen to real people and hear genuine feedback. If the mattress from CloudWorld was too bumpy, the bloggers would put their hands up and tell you it was too bumpy. Now that some blog posts are not always labelled 'sponsored', the reader is none the wiser to whether a review is genuine or paid for. If a company sends a blogger to Hawaii for three weeks all expenses paid, they're hardly going to write a scathing review.

The early noughties was the golden age of blogging. You could create your own thing online and then keep your fingers crossed that someone would pluck you from the masses and offer you a 'proper job'. My blog helped me secure a job working on magazines and then, climbing rung by rung on the ladder, I ended up working at Britain's number-one women's magazine. I was able to show I was already creating content and making my own editorial decisions on my blog. It was the same with Myspace at the time (on a bigger scale). Artists were plucked from there by big production companies: Lily Allen, Kate Nash, Arctic Monkeys and even Adele built up popularity on the social network prior to getting signed. And, of course, young Justin Bieber was catapulted into stardom from his grainy uploads to YouTube. The Internet was a jumping-off point. After all, how can you get anywhere if you don't let people know you exist?

The fact of the matter is that *making my own thing* was the best decision I've ever made. I felt like copying Mark Zuckerberg who apparently used to have business cards that read, 'I'm CEO, bitch', even if I did only have 100 followers. The Internet allows a new kind of freedom where we don't *need* to work the same nine-to-five office jobs any more because we are more connected than ever. Digital nomads write their freelance articles in Bali. Fashion bloggers file their copy from a sun lounger. Students can be taught via webinars. We don't actually work set 'hours' when our emails connect to our phones every two seconds and we check them constantly. We probably work more hours. We are expected to have read the emails on the train, or to have seen the email that came in late on a Sunday night, because we can. We have tools. We have so many tools. But we are still told to work in a job we hate until we die. It doesn't have to be like that. A savvy media type from New York called Dan Schawbel said once: 'Every person is a media company.' Just as you invest in the company you work for – make sure you invest in yourself too.

Fast-forward to 2014. I was at Paddington Station with wet hair, asking for coffee at the Bagel Factory. Two small girls appeared when I turned around, trying not to drop multiple bags.

'Are you Emma?'

'Yes …' I stuttered, suddenly realising how late I was running.

'We love your blog!' they chimed in unison and my face lit up. 'You're one of our favourites!'

I couldn't quite believe that in the middle of London's most hectic train station they'd singled me out and told me they loved my work. It was like magic, because to me my blog felt like such a private corner of the Internet. It suddenly made it all real. It was more than promotion in my 'career'. This was what I'd always wanted – to connect with people through my writing.

It is quite a strange compliment really, because people are essentially saying, 'I like this little space on the Internet that you've constructed for yourself, whether or not it's actually close to your real life.' Because that's all a blog is, a carefully built digital environment, a place you can have a lot of control over. It's your domain name, your rules, your content, your words, your little personal magazine that documents your life. I often wonder if I am 'better' on my blog than in real life. It's definitely prettier and neater than I am. It is also the way I share my soul with the world. Seeing as there are over 150 million blogs on the Internet, for someone to see you and tell you they like yours, well it felt quite amazing.

It took me a while to find people and theories I really responded to, that made me realise that writing creative thoughts online was something to be valued, when conventional capitalist society often feels like it wants to stop pointless creativity. Then all my inspiration came at once when I discovered the likes of Seth Godin, James Altucher, Brené Brown, Liz Gilbert, Cheryl Strayed and Maria Popova. They knocked me over like a set of dominoes. From them I learned the importance of telling and owning your own narrative.

I would always think of that line in *Sister Act 2*, when Whoopi Goldberg is chatting to Lauryn Hill, who is thinking about quitting singing. Whoopi swoops in and explains the quote from Rainer Maria Rilke's *Letters from a Young Poet*: 'If you wake up in the morning and can't think about anything but writing, then you're a writer.' She's comparing it to singing, and I would compare this quote to blogging. A day didn't go by without me thinking about writing on my blog. I started listening to TED Talks that spoke to me about creative confidence, books that spoke to my niggling curiosity, and I soon realised: the reason blogging feels so right is because I believe that a part of me was meant to do this. If you have that euphoric feeling about something, it would be such a shame to try to silence it. I didn't think the world owed me anything, but I owed it to myself to continue doing it for the simple reason that it made me happy.

In Seth Godin's *Stop Stealing Dreams* TEDxYouth talk in 2012 he speaks about how in the 1800s the industrial revolution was the biggest thing to ever happen to the planet. 'It made billions of people rich, it was this engine of productivity and technology working in sync, to mechanise and pave the earth. But in order to do it, you need a hierarchy. A hierarchy involves someone who owns the company or the factory, and everyone else does what they are told [...] it took fifty years to train people to do as they are told.' Obedience used to be a metric of success. Obedience at school. Obedience in the factory. Obedience in the office. Obedience is our parent's generation who work at a company for thirty years. But millennials aren't interested in being obedient. Obedience, to a lot of people now, is the opposite of success. The blogging or freelancer or 'Internet writer' phenomenon of people getting paid to write, review or consult is the result of the Western world no longer needing such a rigid hierarchy – and we can thank the Internet for that. The Internet has killed hierarchy.

And it's not just blogging I'm talking about – I'm talking about people starting their own campaigns on change.org, or writing a viral political article that rivals national newspapers because it catches wind or a social media 'influencer' tweets it, or starting a Kickstarter campaign that leads to a brand-new product or company, or posting a podcast online for anyone in the world to enjoy. By the year 2020, according to Intuit, 40 per cent of the workforce will consist of freelancers and independent consultants. What I'm talking about is the power of self-publishing with no permission needed.

Cutting out the middle-man. Another Seth Godin quote I want on a T-shirt is: *The industry is dead.* I saw this when I started working with brands. They would come directly to me and pay me money to work with them. I didn't have to go through anyone – all I needed was a Wifi connection. What Seth means here is the old 'industries' are dying because artists have direct connections to their audience now. We see this happening with musicians, uploading their music straight to YouTube or SoundCloud. Or celebrities who start their own podcasts or newsletters, like Lenny Letter from Lena Dunham and Jenni Konner. In this post-industrial revolution, obedience isn't a metric of success like it was in the old days. When I started out, even the small act of blogging when I went home made me feel I was rebelling against being indentured to the nine-to-five. It made me feel alive. No permission to be creative was needed.

There are many reasons you might be too scared to start your own thing (website, company, book):

1. You don't have time ('I have kids, a demanding job, loads of other commitments I can't get out of').

2. Your boss won't let you ('my boss is scary, or just might be threatened by my other projects and fire me').

3. You don't have any money ('this project I know won't make money, and I don't have any to start with').

These are all totally legitimate things to feel before starting your own 'thing'. But all these objections listed above come from fear. 'I don't have time' can also mean 'I'm afraid of making time'. It's a sacrifice but there is always time. Elizabeth Gilbert has often shared her book-writing tips, which for her consists of taking half an hour a day with no interruptions, setting an alarm and just *doing* it. Thirty minutes a day. Everyone has at least that. The fear of your bosses not letting you do it is a hard one, I know because I've been there, but it's possible to do things in your spare time and, also, you don't necessarily need to share it with your boss. I used to have a boss who didn't understand how I was able to write an online column for the *Telegraph* in my free time (lunch break and evenings, FYI) while working full-time for her. I thought it was strange: they didn't mind me doing it (they okayed it in a meeting) but they were genuinely confused as to how I found the time. But we all do lots of things in our spare hours: we find the time to have sex, or cook dinner, or go to the gym (sometimes) – so why ask me how I was managing to do extra work? Own the fact that you can find the time that others might not ever make for themselves. And about the money: blogging is *free*. Nothing to lose and so much to gain. Everything wonderful is born of the simple love of doing it.

It was December 2010, and I'd gone along to a Christmas dinner party reunion back home in Exeter at Kate's house. 'This is Emma,' Kate introduced me to some of her friends from university. I always find it interesting how people go about introducing me. This is one of the few ways you can find out what people really think about what you actually 'do' if you don't have a traditional job title. How they'd describe my job would normally vary.

'She writes her feelings on the Internet,' Kate continued. A few people laughed. Not in a mean way, but definitely in an eye-rolling 'what is she like?' sort of way. I would have preferred the label 'entrepreneur' but, you know, can't win them all. A few grey suits lined the dinner table. Most people around the table deli-cately unfolding their napkins across their expensive trousers had Proper Jobs. I was then met with one of my least favourite social situations: small talk.

You'd think I would be quite good at small talk, being someone who works in an industry where I have to strike up new conversa-tions at endless media events or chat with new people on Twitter every day. I *could* talk to a brick wall if I needed to. But whenever anyone comes at me with any sort of weather-related conversation or general chitter-chatter to fill the awkward silence, something inside me conjures a ball of disappointment. This is because I just want to cut to the chase and all of this beating around the bush makes me go funny. What I really want to do in these situations is to ask the other person *real* questions: how are you actually doing? How's your home life? Are you sad? What newspapers do you read? What makes you cackle? Forget the Britishisms about the 'muggy weather': what are *you* actually like? What do you despise? What books are you reading?

Not everyone wants to talk about their feelings all day. Lots of people find my outlook a bit 'much' and slightly exhausting when I bring up something too deep at a light lunch. I was an extremely sensitive child, and often ashamed at how much I *felt*. The responses to my big monologues would be 'you think too much!' or 'try not to get so emotional' or 'things are getting a bit heavy all of a sudden, let's change the conversation!' If I had it my way, I would have got even heavier.

This was my reason for starting a blog. I was surrounded by small talk at parties and media events and I wanted a place in which I could talk about topics that allowed me to think more deeply and discuss ideas with people online who wanted to talk about the same things. I wanted to cover everything from Internet addiction, online dating, death and career anxiety to the highs and lows of being a confused twenty-something who is lucky in so many ways but also feels like the world should feel a little bit sorry for her. The stuff that I hoped no one would read. The stuff I hoped everyone would read. The stuff I would talk about with my friends after two bottles of wine and cry and laugh over.

Maybe in hindsight, that's what I should have called my blog: The Stuff You Can't Talk About at Boring Dinner Parties.

I bought my own domain name (girllostinthecity.com) in 2009, the year before that dinner party in Exeter, for £25. I would come home after feeling guilty about all the rubbish press releases and sales speak I was farming out to people. I think the motivation I had to start the blog was based on guilt. Guilt that I spent 80 per cent of my working week doing something that didn't align with my own morals. I'd see emails going back and forth from brands I admired telling us how to cover up certain fuck-ups and my cheeks would grow hot, knowing that I was involved in things that I couldn't ever tell anyone. For an oversharer like me, it made me constantly feel the need to have an outlet where I could be honest.

I needed that blog like I needed air. I wrote about things that made me feel something, made me happy, made me angry, made me question or ponder over something. As Joan Didion said: 'I write entirely to find out what I'm thinking, what I'm looking at, what I see and what it means. What I want and what I fear.' I'd write to make sense of the world around me. I'd come home after a day of copywriting for a brand of washing detergent and the only way I could lift my soul again was to have a little corner of the Internet that was all mine. I had to save myself by doing something just for me. If it had improved my day even fractionally, it had served its purpose.

But now, fast-forward to 2016 and we're in a Blog Eat Blog world. There are three types of bloggers who big brands are often interested in working with:

1. A blogger with a huge network, but realistically only 25 per cent of their many thousands of followers are real people, as opposed to fake or unused accounts.

2. A blogger with fewer followers than the huge networked bloggers but who is highly influential to a smaller number of people.

3. A blogger who has both of these things. This is the most important type of blogger in brands' eyes. These people have a big network that is full of influential, real people with bank accounts and a relatively high IQ.

Now, I know of lots of bloggers in camps one and two who make a living sponsoring every aspect of their lives. Blogging has evolved to be a money-making machine. Some bloggers have big enough followings for brands to sponsor their weddings, furnish their new flats, pay for them to line up beauty products in their bathrooms, feed their pets, send them on five-star holidays. They might post a picture of an outfit on Instagram and ask you to 'tap for credits!' so that all the brand names appear on their body and a proportion of people looking at that photo will then go on to buy their outfit, and they get a cut of the money. They are like door-to-door salesmen, but it's on Instagram, so it's more like newsfeed-to-newsfeed sales.

I don't need to tell you how powerful that is for brands. A *New York Times* article summed up in 2014 what soon happens to big Internet celebrities: 'Paychecks, or at least free stuff, may follow:

YouTube says thousands of channels in its partner program make six-figure revenues, up 60 per cent over the past year, as intake from mobile ad sales has tripled, while product placement can earn online stars five figures in a few seconds and sponsored tweets thousands of dollars per character.' Anyone could be Internet famous at the beginning. It was ripe for the taking. But Internet fame is becoming harder to achieve because of the sheer *amount* of bloggers out there, all grabbling and fighting for the same opportunities and the same marketing budget.

Influencers are different now. Campaigns are now desperate for clicks, eyeballs, social media impressions and a whole host of varying metrics of success, so asking a traditional celebrity to do a small interview in a local village hall won't convert into straight up sales or awareness in the way it used to. Most old-school celebrities are only just wrapping their heads around Twitter or Facebook and outsourcing it (which isn't really the point of 'social' media).

It's not rocket science that people buy things from sources they trust. Millennials are allergic to bad adverts; it almost has an adverse effect on their buying habits. Well-placed adverts need to be entertaining and correctly placed. It's annoying to have an irrelevant ad in your feed, especially when we give social networks so much of our personal data – there's just no excuse nowadays. Conversely, I have happily watched tons and tons of YouTube pre-roll adverts as if they were normal suggested videos that I would like to watch, because they were good quality, entertaining, clever and well-targeted.

It's not all about blogs now either. People monetise platforms without even needing a website. For example, there are hordes of professional 'Viners' using Twitter's six-second video loop offering, or even 'Periscopers' who use their live-streaming service. I discovered a hilarious girl called 'thejasminator' on Vine recently with 366,000 followers, on average 200,000 loops per video, and she's just a very funny college student dancing in her bedroom. It's short-form. It's addictive. Teenagers are starting to gather big Internet audiences by accident, overnight.

What's nice about having your own 'area' on the Internet is the amount of control we each have over our personal brand. People normally pull a sick face whenever anyone mentions the words 'personal branding.' But a strong personal brand will help someone have more of a pull in the industry over someone without one. Look at the top YouTubers or fashion bloggers: these youngsters have built up huge power bases that now rival magazines that have been around for decades. New digital brands, like Uber or Airbnb, take over, while old brands like Woolworths (RIP) die a death. It's never been easier, for some, to build a brand online that feels like it's been around forever. It's easy to forget old brands too. Old brands need to keep relevant: even Google had to freshen up that logo recently. We expect upgrades – as consumers we don't like complacency – but we don't like too much change either. I'm sure if IKEA changed their colours from yellow and blue we'd flip our lid.

I've always been into the idea of building my own brand. Without really realising it at the time, I have built up my blog as a brand, honing and crafting the things I like and the things that make me *me*. It's important not to take it too seriously, though. You know, like those people you overhear in Starbucks who say stuff like, 'I can't possibly stay in a Travelodge, Kate, it does not align with my #PersonalBrand.' Personal brand snobbery is a thing, and that's not healthy or to be applauded. Having a brand does not mean acting like everything in your life must be controlled or constantly 'on brand' either – we have lives to live. It's just as simple as figuring out Who You Are and What Makes You Different and selling it in to the world. I actively try to stay away from talking about personal branding in a grim 'corporate jargon' type of way – trust me, I've been to enough talks by rich white guys called Tony who tell you to 'Believe in the brand of YOU!' and 'Be the CEO of Company Me, Inc!' I hate those bullshit seminars. I hate jargon of any kind. I do not like it when people say they will 'circle back to me' or 'jump on the line'. I'm a person! I swear! I like emojis! I don't want to talk about evergreen editorial ecosystems! Okay, maybe a bit.

The thing with personal branding is that people assume that they have to construct something perfect – something that they think they should be. That they need to sit down with a big piece of paper and a marker pen and dream up ideas of what their ideal brand should be. That they have to storyboard their Instagram feed. But this should never be the main focus. The main thing to remember is that you are YOU. That is pretty much it. You need to visually or verbally build a space that reflects who you are and what you're good at. Personal branding is a fancy way of saying: 'Here's how I will make you remember me when you're looking for someone to do the job.' The point is that no one else is you. No one else knows what you know from your perspective. No one can write your book. Or tell your story. Or do it like you. The hard part is making people listen, or look up, or remember you.

I market myself every day because I realised early on that my best investment is myself. This can be as simple as telling someone I've just met what I do, where they can find me and offering a card (well, that's quite retro; I normally just swap Twitter names), or linking my blog at the bottom of a magazine article I've written. I have kept my blog name consistent for years over my website,

Twitter, Instagram and Pinterest. I have been in control of all the fonts, photos of myself, things I write, themes, categories and ideas. I have scheduled posts in advance that team up with something timely in the news, or networked with like-minded people with whom I can share ideas. All of these things are the basics for marketing a brand. The rewards of marketing your own name can bring all the cool shit to the yard.

In 2015, a survey revealed that the top career choice for young British people is to be a 'blogger'. A total of 2,348 people were polled as part of the research, all aged between eighteen and twenty-five. Among the reasons given was that 'they get paid good money' and 'they are admired by others'. Back in the day, I'm sure this would been replaced with 'pop star' or 'glamour model' but we're not in the nineties any more – for youths these days it's all about sharing their lives online, whether it's through the kind of blogging/writing that I do or the video incarnation: vlogging.

Vloggers are reality TV stars gone rogue, except they didn't set out to be reality TV stars.

Most people are outwardly confused by this – and others are excited. Vlogging has become the new way to achieve stardom. Girls and boys in their twenties have turned themselves into walking, talking Truman Shows. They have thousands of fans who love them the way I used to love Noel from Hear'Say (I know: what?) – that strange sort of hormonal love. That 'I would die for you' sort of love, which years later you think was a tad dramatic.

The new Internet stars are camera-ready as soon as they open their eyes each morning, with great skin and lovely speaking voices. They are sharing every single element of their lives. We've seen vloggers come out for the first time to their viewers before they have to their own families, we've seen baby announcements, we've seen vloggers having breakdowns, we've seen arguments between well-known bloggers on Twitter. We've seen everything.

But have we?

Ironically, we don't see much at all. We don't see someone's life; they're not in a goldfish bowl being filmed live as they are in *Big Brother*. There is an argument to be made that we are not our true selves on social media. We are clever, us humans, we know exactly what we're sharing and how we want to be perceived. We've already pre-empted the response to our funny tweet before we've sent it. We create a funny sentence in our head and save it in our drafts for the perfect moment. We are curating our beautiful lives each day.

It goes back to this idea that it's all about having your own brand. Obviously it's important to actually be good at what you do too; I would hate for kids to think that 'followers' are the only thing that matters. On the Project Casting website a talent agent admitted to saying 'Instagram followers are more important than acting talent', which made me frown hard. According to a September 2015 report by *Variety*, talent agencies and casting directors are ditching retro open-casting calls and scouring for talent on Vine, YouTube and Twitter for the next leading acting role. Mitch Gossett said in the article: 'If you have two clients up for the same part and one has 6 million followers and one has 27 (followers), they're going to give it to the one with 6 million followers because of the direct access to promotion that will cost them nothing.' Welcome to the future, kids.

Divided opinions to one side, YouTubers deserve to be acknowledged for this bizarre shift in the media landscape. Right now we're in a strange no man's land of Internet freedom vs newspapers freaking out about their commercial objectives. Men in grey suits are getting annoyed. They don't like change. Whereas us millennials, we LOVE trying new things. Why are the newspapers and advertising networks suddenly all over the YouTubers like a rash? Because the fun and frivolous YouTuber crew can sell things.

And they can do it well because they're not asking and they don't have an agenda. It's the result of a snowball effect, and this is the beauty of the shift. It's totally based on a voluntary audience. These fans subscribe because they want to, and they call the tune.

YouTubers sell things based on customer demand. *Write a book please. We want to see this type of video next. Can you film something with your sister? Bring out a bubble bath range! Come to Ireland. Sell some T-shirts with your face on.* They respond to the requests of their massive and loyal community. This is something a lot of traditional companies could learn from.

The media world has changed and is changing and will change again. Vlogging is the new blogging: it's an interesting format to consume when there is nothing on TV. We stream, we play, we pause, we listen, we watch three screens at once. We show a clip of YouTube to a friend on our phone, while they're on their laptop, while we're both watching TV. This is life now.

The point of all of this is that we all have our channels, our own means of communication. You. Your friends. These YouTubers. These Vines or blog posts are really no different from watching *You've Been Framed* or watching some of the housemates on *Big Brother* plait each other's hair in the diary room, except the content we see isn't being determined by a corporation. These twenty-somethings deliver their lives straight to our laptops. Mark Zuckerberg made a billion dollars all because he realised human beings are really bloody nosy. We want to know what other people's kitchens look like. We want to know if someone is happy or depressed, and the reasons for both. We want to know what people have in their fridge.

It's still slightly jarring and a bit off-kilter to see 'Internet celebs' in the mainstream media. I guess it's always interesting when national newspapers suddenly cotton on to things. (It's always a bit late, too.) Things continue to evolve slowly and grow in popularity, but when a new thing reaches the mainstream, the papers jump all over it. But ironically the technology and popularity of blogging has evolved to the point of being a true competitor to traditional media. The YouTube and blogging crew have been in this game for years and now it's all paying off. And to anyone who has a voice and Wifi connection, that's exciting.

I am a fan of any millennial who has made a job out of a new industry. The reason I am pro-YouTubers isn't necessarily just because of the content they create. It's more because I admire their entrepreneurial mindset and the way they have been in charge of their own editorial content and made a name for themselves in a new, exciting way. Anyone who does something that bypasses 'the old way of doing it' totally gets my vote. So many companies are becoming stale because they refuse to wake up to how quickly the Internet changes month on month and how people consume things nowadays. Claudia Oshry founded the popular Instagram @ girlwithnojob and now, ironically, Instagram *is* her full-time job. She monetises her feed and was nominated for a People's Choice award. The traditional media outlets may be cynical, but there's no doubting that this girl is smart.

The new Internet stars are curating, filming, writing, editing, recording, creating assets, coming up with ideas, working with brands and publishing their own material. I think that's more impressive than working for an establishment that is stuck in its ways and frightened of change. We should we supporting those millennials who have made a business for themselves using whatever tools and skills they have.

On the flipside, a piece on the US website The Hairpin in 2015 made my ears prick up. Discussing 'success' in the Internet age, a writer called Jamie Keiles described it as being 'when I can sustain a career without being on Twitter … I would love to someday be able to get work and have readers without regularly exposing myself online as totally thirsty for work'. This made me nostalgic for days when people didn't need to tout their wares publicly all the time. In an interview in the *NME*, Noel Fielding says it's not the cool thing to do: 'Me and Julian [Barratt from *The Mighty Boosh*] are from a different generation, where it's embarrassing to promote yourself. If you walk into a shop and go, "Hey, who likes my trousers?" most people will go, "Mate, you're a dick." So why say it on Twitter?'

So what is success in the Internet age? Of course, it means different things to different people, but maybe putting a success metric on 'followers' is dangerous. Treating social media like a numbers game will only end in tears. Chasing clicks will leave us hollow. Creating meaningful content that people enjoy will make the difference. Social media can be fantastic if we keep it real. It is not healthy to rate people like they are an item on Amazon. By all means, create what you love, but without the need to feel validated by numbers. The number of people following your life does not define who you are. You are more than your social media accounts, more than your job, more than your followers.

'Nothing of me is original. I am the combined effort of everyone I've ever known.'

Chuck Palahniuk

chapter 10
If Tinder Was For Friendships

2012

You don't find your best friends overnight. They don't get mailed to you in the post after ordering them online. You don't find them hiding under a rock, or in a cupboard under the stairs, or waiting patiently on a train platform holding a coffee-with-one-sugar-and-skimmed-milk just how you like it. No one sidles up next to you and hands you half of a Best Friends Forever necklace while they clutch the other half without you proving yourself first; you have to work hard for that cheap piece of jewellery. The mission is to go out into the world and seek them out.

Here is my Friendship Pyramid:

1. Best friends, who are just there, all the time. You never leave each other alone. You have pointless chats in WhatsApp groups

that constantly drain your battery and make you snort on public transport.

2. Mates that you love and will always be on any party invite list. They are great for getting drunk with and you would describe them as fun and 'good value'.

3. Brand new mates who you are excited about getting to know aka 'Honeymoon Friends'.

4. Coffee once a month friends who you both wish you saw more of, but actually, you both know that the reason you like each other is because you hardly see each other.

5. People who you've known for years, who only get in touch when they want something – you feel indebted to them because you've got 'history'.

6. The-Ghosts-Of-Friendship Past who only say 'happy birthday' on your Facebook wall or worse, just 'HB'.

7. People who you bump into and awkwardly say 'let's do coffee!' in a high-pitched nervous voice and you both know you NEVER ever will.

As the years have gone by, I've come to realise that you have different friends for different reasons, and perhaps different parts of your life. Some people have ended up being a bit of a 'rent-a-friend' – both of us being unsure of who is renting each other – but they are there for a limited period of time, not forever. Others are knitted into the fabric of your life in a lifelong agreement.

I found mine by accident. On odd years, even years, up and down years, unusual situations and unexpected occasions. Some of my best girls who are the most loyal, caring friends in the world actually bullied me and put rocks in my bag when we were about twelve or thirteen years old. I know, talk about a plot twist. One day they were whispering about me, and then a week later they jumped out from behind a sofa and shouted 'joke!' and we were all suddenly best mates – and we still are.

Often on paper a friendship doesn't quite add up. You're like two clashing algorithms on a dating site; you're too similar, or you're too different. For example, I am a social media addict (and it is my job, to be fair) and my best and oldest friend Charlotte has sent about two tweets in her life and her username has about eight numbers following it reminiscent of a nineties Hotmail email address. Her technical inabilities make me laugh. But opposites do attract and something ignites, followed by an intense, almost romantic friendship. It might be sparked by something as small as both wondering whatever happened to Phats & Small and then spending the whole afternoon re-playing their one hit 'Turn Around' and taking videos of each other dancing to it. Only Charlotte would reply like it was the most normal thing in the world when I asked her to come round and record a video of us both mouthing the lyrics to Nicki Minaj's 'Superbass'.

There's a famous quote by motivational speaker Jim Rohn that claims you are the average of the five people you spend the most time with. Whenever I come across this idea, I think: 'Well, that's GOOD. Because my friends are exactly who I want to be, that's why I picked them in my squad.' I want to be more like all my friends for different reasons. I think they are better humans than I am. My best friend Charlotte is tidier and more thoughtful than me, and looks after her clothes like they are people. My other best friend Emma is a great cook and the most hospitable person I know – her extrovert personality makes her the perfect dinner-party host, whereas I just want people to leave immediately. And my third, Polly, is more grown-up than me; she is getting married and is a responsible chic adult who wears expensive jewellery and has an important job in fashion and a grown-up haircut. My friend Georgie is hard as nails but, equally, knows when you just need to lie in bed together, feeling sad, in silence, with a cup of tea and wearing a disgusting hoody.

There is something so wonderfully complex about labelling someone a 'best friend'. It is leaps ahead of 'friend', who is just someone you like a bit without a special kind of bond tying you together like you are white-water rafting through life with each other. It's a commitment, for starters, but one that you can't ever imagine not being part of. You fall quite romantically for each other and think: 'Yep, you. You will soon become an extension of my personality; I will finish your sentences and you will know all my most awful secrets, and therefore hold all the power over me for ever more. And, oh balls, I can never ever forget your birthday.'

A best friend combines so many relationships in one: Emma often nurtures me like a mother, hoovering under my feet and telling me off for being messy. With Charlotte, on the other hand, we would go on a crazy night out in our nearest seaside town, lose our shoes on the beach and then snuggle up and spoon each other to sleep. There'd be times when she'd drunkenly pass out topless with a Clean & Clear wipe on her face and I'd wake up with her boob stuck to my shoulder. That's the thing about best friends: it is an intensity and closeness that can make you feel like you're literally sharing the same brain. It's the 'half of me is missing' feeling when they go away for long periods of time. It's the private jokes that literally no one else would get. And it's the sudden rage during an argument when you want to push them over and scream at them for hurting you. But that's okay, because you know you'll make up a few minutes later. You realise that you love each other not for each other's achievements, but just because you do, and always will, for no real reason.

It's the pep talks, the 'you can do it' Post-its on the fridge, the shared rebellion of having a sneaky cigarette on a Sunday night before bed and laughing as you 'put the world to rights'. It's the making of a cup of tea when you didn't ask for one. It's the 'I F*CKING LOVE YOU' texts at 3 a.m. It's quoting the same thing from *The Emperor's New Groove* a hundred times, and it never gets old. It's when you're with other people's mates and you find yourself thinking *you're not as good as mine*. It's the stuff they know about you when you were fifteen and chubby. It's the silence when you're sad, the shouting when you're angry. It's the 'I'm-so-pissed-off-with-you-but-I-can't-stay-angry-because-this-really-funny-thing-happened-today-and only-you-will-understand-It'. It's the crawling into their bed when you're hungover, and hating yourself and the world. It's the lending of money when you have a shit internship and can't afford milk. It's the telling you off for being out of order. It's the times when they do your washing-up, and it's the times you realise that actually you need to do the washing-up because you should stop taking your friend for granted.

I've also come to realise that you are who you follow. In real life and online. This means keeping close the people who make you a better person, like a shepherd herding his precious flock, and moving away from others who don't. It's a brave thing to rid yourself of people who seem to only add drama or sadness to your life. I've phased out a lot of people who were once my friends, and I'm certain that a lot of people have done that to me too. I regret a few people I phased out, such as my course friend and editor of my university magazine who pulled my write-up about Michael Jackson at the last minute without telling me. I'd spent all summer writing and editing it so I never spoke to her again. People *know* when something means a lot to you. I was a dramatic nineteen-year-old and I couldn't take any chances on someone who would cut out my article and then avoid me.

In the last few years I've added some incredible people to my friendship circle by meeting them on social networks. It always happens organically. By living our real selves online and searching for things we love, it is easy to cross paths with new people and form niche friendships. My friendships online have occurred because I am at a point in my life where I know who I am, what I like and what I'm trying to achieve. Of course, I've also got it wrong in the past too, thinking that someone is a certain thing but subsequently realising they aren't. It's easy to make mistakes on the Internet. Turns out you can get platonically catfished, too.

For me it's important to create a healthy environment for yourself online – and that means surrounding yourself with people who bring out the best in you. Life's too short to be dragged down by following the thoughts of negative people. You are what you read. Before you know it, their anger or negativity will seep into your frontal lobes and you'll be a cynical robot too in no time. Watch out for positivity zappers! For this reason I decided to unfollow anyone who tweets too dramatically: 'My bread-making machine is broken, I WANT TO DIE' or 'I hate …' too many times a day, or if they complain about being bored. I decided to also unfollow people who were seemingly giving themselves a hernia over transport issues, screeching at a train or plane company publicly in fifty separate tweets.

In a nutshell I decided to mute people who are *constantly outraged by small things*. It was starting to have an effect on me, and making me anxious for no reason. This is because in my opinion you cannot get to the crux of an issue or have valuable conversations when either person is angry. I wouldn't befriend someone in real life who was just reeling off curse word after curse word of mouthy abuse so I don't tend to be drawn towards it online either. Writing ALL IN CAPITALS is cute if it's your grandpa trying to text, but it's not such a good look on an angry Twitter-dwelling keyboard warrior. It's not the basis for a good conversation, either. A dialogue that already starts off angry means people act out of turn, or they feel their issue is the only issue, or they say things they don't mean. You have to at least go into the conversation in a neutral non-caps-lock state of mind. I think it's always best to have a little simmer down, and then have a chat, human to human.

Via the Internet I have connected with people who really inspired me, made me think, gave things meaning, and encouraged me to think more deeply about world issues, without being aggressive in the process. These are all people I have added to my Internet tribe. One of my favourite 'thinkers', Seth Godin, describes tribes in this way: 'Founded on shared ideas and values, tribes give ordinary people the power to lead and make big change.' A friend, who I met online, defines them as more along the lines of 'soul-sisters-who-are-on-your-side-whatever-the-fuck-happens'. To me, that is a tribe.

Thinking about it, I always enjoyed the 'meeting up with strangers' aspect of Internet dating, but now I'm in a relationship that path is closed to me. (I've actually always wished someone would invent the 'friends' equivalent to Tinder. I would love to be able to search in a square-mile radius for someone who is algorithmically like-minded and not an axe-murderer to have a cup of tea and chat.) But Twitter actually kind of turned into Tinder for me, except for friendship dating, and I have met so many cool new people through it, many of whom have turned into IRL friends.

I love the fact that you can pretty much filter through people online to find your perfect friend 'matches'. Similar interests, topics, like-minded followers, conversations and hashtags are now bringing us closer together, and it's a beautiful thing (an example of algorithms being a good thing!). If you are supposedly meant to be able to find your sexual soulmate online then why can't you have loads of nice new friendships too? Plus, anyone that thinks they already 'have enough friends, thanks' obviously hasn't experienced their first 'friend crush' online, which according to good old Urban Dictionary is when you 'experience a strong desire to become friends with a person you don't know very well'. I get these a lot. I fall in love with potential new friends every day on my different social newsfeeds.

Through Twitter, I've also found out about and still go to 'supper clubs', like the infamous Clapton Pot in Hackney, where strangers meet up for dinner. We were told the dining table was down some rickety stairs ('you'll have to take your heels off to get down there,' they said), and for a moment I had fear in my eyes. Had we thought we were joining a 'supper night' with strangers when in fact we were going to get lured down into the basement to be murdered or kept as prisoners? Turned out that the two hosts were amazing – they laid on the best food and wine ever – and we're still in touch now. I heard some of the most interesting stories that night. Stories from a man who worked at the BBC, a couple who had moved over from Australia, and a detailed historical timeline of the Hackney road we were on, from someone who had lived there their whole lives. Turned out having dinner in a stranger's basement was pretty cool.

Despite the benefits of occasions like these, I still feel slightly judged whenever I explain that I actively seek out ticketed events in which I go to a stranger's house. When I tell my IRL friends down the pub that I've been for dinner with two girls I met on the web, it has sometimes been clear my IRL friends thought it was slightly strange.

'You what? Like, you met with two strangers from the Internet? For dinner? BUT WHY? Were we busy? Are you *okay*?'

But it wasn't technically true that they were 'strangers' just because I hadn't met up with them yet. I'd been exchanging links, LOLs and one-liners with these girls for months, plus we had heaps of mutual friends in the media industry – so what was weird about that? We had so much in common, it was like we'd known each other for years.

Similarly I've noticed that having lots of 'online friends' still comes with its own raised eyebrow. Why don't you just hang out with your *real friends*? Isn't that enough? Why do you go seeking strangers so much?

When I asked on Twitter who had met their best friend online I received endless replies. In fact my laptop momentarily crashed because I got hundreds of direct messages. Here are some ways people told me they'd made friends online: a woman called Sam told me she'd met her best friend via a fortnightly podcast they both contributed to – it was like having regular public phone calls, and after meeting up offline they became best friends. Internet writer Jamie Varon met her best friend on Twitter and via blogs: after twenty-four hours they realised they were pretty much the same person and decided to live together. Bee Barker told me she met her best friend on LiveJournal, which was an online diary-keeping community that she was super-active on a few years back. Stéphanie told me she'd met her BFF Esther on a virtual game called Habbo Hotel, and they then found each other again in the comment section of Zoella's YouTube channel, which is when they became really close friends. Jess said she'd met her friend Mandy on Instagram – they'd attended a local event (separately), and when they both posted to Instagram, they used the same hashtag. The next day, they were perusing through the posts, came across and followed each other, which then turned into a proper friendship. A lady called Regina emailed me to say she'd met her husband and best friend on the now-defunct Yahoo Groups in 1998. It was a group based on swing music and dancing.

I also asked my friend the YouTuber Zoe Sugg (aka Zoella) about her best friend who she met online. Her reply: 'I met Louise Pentland (sprinkleofglitter) via email because she used to read my blog and wanted to tell me she loved it, and then later we spoke every day on MSN, which slowly progressed to Skype. In real life we met at a beauty blogger event and automatically shared a lot of interests – beauty, blogging, photography – and so we always had things to talk about but I also just found her so entertaining and warm. We instantly clicked and it was like we'd known each other forever.'

I don't exactly know how I stumbled across the strobe light that is Laura Jane Williams. But, in February 2014, she'd written an article for the *Huffington Post* called 'Nine Lady Blogs You Should Be Reading' and I was included in it. It was a lovely compliment and we started chatting online. I'd already been following her tweets from afar. We starting direct messaging, then tweeting, and then one day a mutual friend of ours organised a night out to drink and talk about writing, blogging and general life. We met in person; she was wearing a black hat and buttoned-up denim shirt and I had just dyed my hair purple and wasn't feeling it. I was praying she wouldn't judge me for my new goth hair. We chatted and chatted and I went home with my iPhone notes full of books and articles that she had recommended to me. It's totally possible to fall for someone's brain, and that's what happened here. Everything she was saying was so *interesting* to me. I was glued to her.

Laura had quit her job, or in fact been 'let go' (I hate that phrase – sounds like you've let go of a rope: so long, sucker!), but she saw this as a sign to do something bigger, something she'd always wanted to do but had been too scared to make the transition. This was the Laura frame of mind: turning something that looked a bit shit on paper and making it into something go-getting. I admired her ability to turn a bad situation into a positive one. She took an unknown leap and went travelling, to earn money from Internet writing abroad and to attempt the digital nomad lifestyle. She actually turned her 'fuck-it-just-do-it' learnings into an e-book called *The Book of Brave*.

The thing about putting yourself, your words and your life on the Internet also means you get 'unwelcome guests' like nits; they come and rock up in places that comfort you and temporarily turn it into a dark and miserable place. The Internet calls them 'trolls'.

I found myself talking about this excessively to Laura. She understood how it was possible to gather a crop of people who didn't like you or your outlook on life. She got it – because she was muddling in the shit with me. It really helped to be able to talk to someone who understood. Who got how much it hurts when someone criticises you and your work, even if it is just a tweet, a blog post found on the fiftieth page of Google or a forum of haters. Laura was entrenched in the world of writing on the Internet and we were both building our own tribes and communities. Together, when hashing out our pretty niche 'life goals', no amount of negativity around us mattered. We also had a similar purpose: to connect with other individuals who light our souls on fire and push ourselves further each day; to be unabashedly ourselves in our careers and personal lives.

Laura and I, over the course of our friendship, have made each other braver. Sharing each other's work, cheerleading each other's achievements, building a crew of creative people around us, meeting up for monthly group dinner dates. (Laura would email saying 'I've booked it under my name, I thought "Badass Bitches From The Internet" would be a bit much.')

When I think of Laura, and my other 'Internet Friends', I think of Shine Theory, a term coined by American writer Ann Friedman. Friedman's 2013 piece in *New York Magazine's* The Cut website summed this theory up as being the 'I don't shine if you don't shine' rule of thumb and it came with some advice: 'when you meet a woman who is intimidatingly witty, stylish, beautiful, and professionally accomplished, befriend her. Surrounding yourself with the best people doesn't make you look worse by comparison. It makes you better.' Laura's confidence, honesty, writing talents and ability to 'work the room' made me want to instantly befriend her. And it made me better. These women who I would have observed and seen as a 'threat' back in my insecure days started becoming my best mates.

A year later, in 2015, in a café in Stoke Newington, Laura and I had this crazy idea that we should launch a networking panel event for women. The women we'd tweeted, yet never met. We knew so many women via their cool profile pictures and bios but we realised that we'd spent too long talking in 140 characters – we wanted to get everyone offline and into a room. We called it 'IRL: a live panel event for women off the Internet'. We had no funding and no real experience in 'events', but in just over a week we built a custom-made website, bespoke newsletter, Eventbrite page and even persuaded Twitter to allow us to launch the event at their headquarters. We hosted 100 women in one room, most of whom we'd never met before, and we trended in the UK on Twitter, reaching 5 million eyeballs on social media. I could never have done that on my own. This was definitely Shine Theory at work. We'd successfully hosted a In-Real-Life-Party for 100 new potential friends.

As we grow older, we realise that our personalities are a reflection of who we spend our time with, online and offline. One of my favourite writers, Ryan O'Connell, once wrote that your twenties is 'like a friendship massacre. There is blood all over the walls'. He's right you know. You cannot do everything you are doing and keep all of those friends you've accumulated from the last twenty-plus years. It's physically and literally impossible. Meeting new friends through Twitter and blogs has really added value to my life, as opposed to scouring through the dreaded Facebook timeline only to see a girl from primary school announcing that she's 'hung out her washing to dry and has had a really good day!' When you grow up, have bills to pay, start working in a strenuous, emotionally draining job, especially one you love, time is suddenly way more precious. Why would you go for a coffee with someone you don't really know or like when you haven't even had the time to catch up with your own mother for yonks? The weeks are long and busy with a tiny slither of light that is used as one's 'spare time'. We don't have time to drag along a dying friendship any more. The statistics say that the average person has 157 Facebook 'Friends' in the UK, but I think we can all call bullshit on that. We all know who the real ones are – whether we found them online or offline.

'The problem of abuse is the greatest challenge the web faces today.'

Umair Haque, 2015

chapter 11
They Don't Just Exist in Fairy Tales

2013

Dear Troll,

You know it's all real, don't you? You, your keyboard, your words – it's real to someone. That very same night you posted your abuse, I went to the pub with my boyfriend and spoke about you. You are anonymous – but I now feel different and not as good in my new denim dungarees. I was laughing earlier – now I'm paranoid. Could you be an anonymous person in this pub? Why is that man looking at me weirdly? Why did that woman scowl at me on the way in? I feel suddenly fragile and violated. Tears. Empty red wine glasses. The songs play in the background and smoke drifts in from the smokers' den outside.

Am I really like that? Am I really that person? So why did you say all that stuff?

Troll, you make people question themselves, and they don't even know you. Your comments don't evaporate into thin air. It's not 'laughed off' or 'swept under the rug' or turned into a revengeful work of art. Even if a 'block' button is pressed or the recipient tries strategies to shake it all off psychologically, it still leaves an invisible stamp. A mark. A little stain left on someone's heart that will take a while to scrub off, like a dodgy henna tattoo on a package holiday.

Your comment took five seconds to type and send, but it will take a long time to vanish from the memory of whoever received it. That is how human beings work. This is how it will always work. We always remember the negative things because they so often hit us on a bruise we already have, or a wound that has not yet totally healed. We remember criticism and heartache. Compliments fade away more quickly because we don't believe them as much. Compliments aren't as sticky. Compliments sometimes just flop on the floor, like soggy pasta.

The Internet makes things seem so flimsy, so temporary, with a hurtful comment being easily physically deleted, but it never properly is, because the words and feelings always linger. It doesn't matter about it still being seen online, because the words are already stamped in the person's head. Your hateful words cut through my computer screen. I don't want this mess to be public.

I shouldn't have to delete myself even though you're making me want to.

This isn't trolling. It is abuse.

Emma

It's a bit weird that we call them 'trolls'. Troll is a funny word. It's one of those nineties toys with the crazy purple hair, or it's a fairytale character under a bridge hanging out with a couple of goats. But a 'troll' is something we also call a real person, whether it's a twelve-year-old in their bedroom messing around or an adult who thrives off throwing viral hate bombs towards others on the Internet.

From a very young age I noticed a pattern in Disney films. I probably should have just been getting lost in Ariel's 'Part of Your World' and singing it into a plastic microphone but instead I wrote in my diary in the worst handwriting: 'Dear Diary, in all my favourite films there are always baddies.' I found this page in my oldest diary (I wrote this when I was nine) and it couldn't be truer to my twenty-six-year-old self. *There are always baddies. Even in the favourite parts of my life.* That might have been the one realistic thing that Disney taught me. One minute you're hanging out with your two mates (Flounder and Sebastian) and then a sea witch comes along and ruins everything.

I've often heard people say that their trolls highlighted what they had feared in themselves the most. This made me wonder if trolls only have power if you already believe what they have to say. Whether the troll only exists if you let it. Maybe they *are* mythical. Maybe the only reason people give their trolls the time of day is because they are a digital version of the everyday demons we have inside our heads anyway. I often think I used to be my own troll – the amount of mean stuff I used to say to myself in the mirror. If another person had say it, my friends would have jumped to my defence. But it was inside my own head.

My favourite response to a troll has to be that of J. K. Rowling, who once received the tweet: 'Is Rowling angling for some online abuse? Must have a new book/play/film in the pipeline. Publicity.' To which J. K. Rowling replied: 'God knows how Harry Potter got so big! I could go weeks at a time without being called a quisling whore in the nineties.' This exchange made me roll my eyes (at the troll) and smile (at her reply), and it really made me think. Before the Internet, before online trolls, we could just get on with our lives and make the work we wanted to make without any strange comebacks.

Of course, not everyone is the powerhouse that is J. K. Rowling. But this is not to assume she is invincible. Even the biggest of celebrities or public figures find trolling hard to deal with. That is the unfortunate assumption that some people make about celebrities online, the 'they can take it' attitude. No one should *take* it. But it interesting that perhaps younger celebrities who have grown up with social media perhaps *expect it* a bit more. Lena Dunham once said: 'Celebrities can complain all they want about how cruel Twitter is, but we signed up for it. Who didn't sign up for it are the teenage girls who bully each other to suicide using Twitter.' No one deserves to be a victim of online abuse for deciding to freely live their lives. But by watching our celebrities deal with haters, at least the rest of Twitter is able to learn from them. Watching how Lena deals with Internet shit-storms has made me feel stronger, as she so honestly admits how easy it is for social networks to turn ugly. One good thing is that your sisterhood will always have your back.

Here are some tips I've gathered along the way, if you are to acquire a little troll:

1. As Caitlin Moran does, reply to horrible tweets with 'your mum'.

2. Send them a GIF of a panda snuggling another panda.

3. As a friend of mine recently did, just type: 'Oh piss off and eat a Jaffa cake.'

4. Go and get a hug from someone who loves you even when you've got greasy hair.

5. The best tip? DON'T ENGAGE.

Being on the Internet all day crossing paths with Tom, Dick or Harry could be damaging to your mental health if you're letting in things that might harm you. I wasn't affected too badly – I had a cry and I leaned on my friends to distract me – but the knock-back that I personally felt from my trolls made me question whether the Internet is a good thing for creative people. Creative people, after all, are extremely sensitive. If you want to create things sometimes you don't want immediate feedback. If you are an artist of some sort – a musician, author, painter, sculptor or illustrator – it's a long process to get to a place in which you are ready to release your creation into the world, and prepared to hear the response. Everything is instant now. Someone can tell you they hate or love your thing so quickly. Some things need to be separated from the creator, at least for a small amount of time. Sometimes, the Internet does not always allow people to think out loud in case they get something wrong.

I have nostalgic fantasies of the olden days. I long to go back and ask the famous names of the past how they got on with their life's work: a bit like Owen Wilson did in *Midnight in Paris*. I love the idea that Shakespeare sweated away with a quill for hours and then, once his work was penned, people saw his plays and discussed it down the tavern, and that was that. The reaction would be from real people, real crowds. He didn't have to deal with aggressive tweets, or passive-aggressive comments on his blog or people telling him to die in the *Guardian* comments section. He'd just get some hecklers in the crowd in real life and then he could probably just go home to a cup of broth. This made me think it was probably a good thing that J. K. Rowling wasn't knee-deep in social media back when she was writing her Harry Potter series. Now, after Harry has been out in the world for years, she can be Queen of Twitter by responding to fans directly via that medium, making up extra little parts of the story for her most avid readers – 140-character extensions of her books. I think social media is wonderful for that. However, I cannot imagine that Twitter would have been a good thing to check in on actually during the original creative process; would *you* want the constant feedback? Sometimes I believe an author or artist does need to step away from the Internet and practise their craft on their own. But it's hard because, let's be honest: now we have it, it's difficult to stay away.

At the Edinburgh Fringe Festival, I went along to see a performance by a stand-up comedian I admire. The subject matter of her show was very bold, and with confidence she gave the crowd her opinions on rape, abortion, feminism and racism. She turned her viewpoints into creative comedy – either punchy one-liners or mini sketches that poked fun at how corrupt the world can be, and how ridiculous some people's attitudes are. She was brave, her eyes were sparkling and she was feeding off the gasps and shocked faces of the crowd. When I saw her second show, I was expecting the same sort of wow factor, or maybe even something to top it. She was one of the bravest comedians I'd even seen perform. I nudged my boyfriend, warning him that he was in for a real treat, and to brace himself for some seriously thought-provoking scenes.

But instead, I was surprised to find that most of her show mainly focused on the subject of Internet trolls. Instead of her ballsy, opinionated show, she gave her stage time to the trolls who had offended her. Her eyes weren't at all sparkly. Her trolls ran her show. I couldn't help but reflect on the irony of this. It seemed as though this wasn't her art any more. She'd been hijacked without realising it. Maybe like this chapter of my book.

There are two (main) types of Internet uproar:

1. Disagreement: people just disagree with you. Get over it. You are not Jesus.

2. Trolling: horrible, offensive and often illegal behaviour. Sometimes even death and rape threats.

I'll tell you an example of a disagreement: in 2011 I accidentally offended loads of people. Well, in hindsight it wasn't that accidental, it was quite clear that I was being out of order. My points were worded badly. I'd made a mistake. I wasn't yet skilled enough to portray my thoughts in the right way. This was the danger of experimenting with online pieces for a company website when I'd had no real hands-on experience at all. On your own freshly made blog with a small audience it's fine to say what you want, but on a huge public platform you're asking for trouble. I was still in my first job and I'd written something I didn't *technically mean* for a website with millions of readers.

Let me rewind a little. I'd just been accepted as a London representative for a well-known American website for women which had lots of traffic and lots of extremely engaged followers. Each article I wrote would get heaps of comments and I really enjoyed the community engagement and responding to people's opinions. I was so super-happy to be writing for them and I realised that what I wanted more than anything else was to be a writer on the Internet. The dream was happening.

So, one weekend I went to a comedy festival in the deepest, darkest British countryside. We huddled inside the tent, with beer and blankets, and settled in to have a good old laugh. But sadly, in all honesty, I didn't enjoy the stand-up comedians I saw. There were three female comedians. None of them made me laugh once. It seemed try-hard, fake and bitchy. I was disappointed that I didn't find them funny. My boyfriend had not moved his facial muscles during the hour either. We just didn't laugh.

During the sets, each comedian either put on baby voices or they bitched about how shit it was being a woman; one shared the ups and downs of finding a wedding dress, the other said that girls in short skirts were asking for it. I was taken aback and upset. The three comedians had pretty much covered just three topics: marriage, babies or being a wife. It was the age-old stereotype, that women could only joke about one thing (being a woman) whereas men could joke about anything they wanted to.

I turned to my boyfriend: 'I don't get this. Like, men have always had free rein to talk about whatever they want – one guy's set was just about him going to Curry's to buy a hoover – yet women seem to feel boxed in to only talking about certain women-related issues. Why is that? I think I'll pitch the idea to the magazine I'm writing for. See what they think.'

Normally my articles were a little lighter, along the lines of 'fifteen amazing moments from Mary-Kate and Ashley films of the past!' but this time I thought I'd take on these comedians for not being funny. In my article I started slamming into one of the comedians from the opening line. I was doing the worst thing you can possibly do: I was generalising carelessly about something based on one experience.

It began:

'The main reason [the comedian's] stand-up act aggravated me (and pretty much everyone there, judging by the amount of people leaving the tent) was that she spoke about "women's issues".'

Putting 'women's issues' in quote marks sounded a bit misogynistic.

'Her introduction launched into ripping apart women who have sex too much. Then onto pregnancy, then divorce and back into taking out young girls in tiny shorts. All of her "funny" material was just about women.'

Again … this reads like I hate women.

'Why do you female comedians have to talk about these same topics? It makes us women look like we have nothing else to talk about. That we moan all the time about being a woman. We're not just baby-making machines who complain about shoes and diets. At least I don't think so. Where's the broader material?'

I didn't stop there, though.

'Men don't just talk about weight problems, or penis size, or diets, or how insecure they feel at the gym. They talk about objects, experiences, funny moments, observations. For the most part, their material remains gender neutral.'

Oh my God, I can't believe I wrote this.

I was basically saying that men were funny and women weren't, simply because these three particular comedians' material had been about women or womanhood. It was clear what had happened here: a) I'd been brainwashed and had absorbed the way that men speak about women (and how the media treat women in general) and echoed it back through my own voice, and b) I'd assumed that comedy could only be funny if it's non-gender-specific. I was not self-aware. I wasn't being fair either. I also had no right to take down these women for on that day deciding to talk about being female.

The next day I receive an email, from the website's editor.

Hey Emma,

I had to pull your piece that went up today. I wasn't going to post it at first (and really shouldn't have), as it's derisive of females in the arts, which is sort of our whole site's purpose. That's not to say that we don't accept our writers' opinions and they can't differ, but ultimately if I'd left it up I think this piece would have caused more uproar than genuine conversation.

Let me know if you have any other questions – I'll be glad to talk to you more about it.

Thanks,

Kate

I was devastated. 'More uproar than genuine conversation' – oh my God, I thought, *I am the troll*. My piece had its own think-pieces written about it. My Twitter newsfeed was on fire with people hating me and hating my writing. 'I can't believe someone paid her to write this,' said one. 'I wish I'd never known this person existed,' wrote another.

Re-reading my piece years later, through my fingers, it was crystal clear how much more I've learned about the world around me and how easy it can be to take a wrong stance that later makes you cringe. My argument reads like internalised misogyny. Men have hated female comedy for as long as anyone can remember, and there I was in a male-dominated comedy tent judging these women for 'not being funny' because they weren't talking about 'things that men find funny'.

A few years later, I came across an interview with Ellen DeGeneres on the Makers Women network in which she speaks about how her comedy in her early career was different because she didn't focus specifically on being a woman: 'It was an odd thing for a woman to be a comedian, number one, and then to be a comedian in the way I chose to tell jokes, which was non-gender-specific. I didn't ever do "ladies am I right?" or "that time of the month". Mainly because I was gay and I didn't focus on the difference between men and women.' But this brought it home to me even more: each person is different. Everyone's story is different. We can't make up rulebooks for people or waggle a finger whenever we disagree with someone's choices.

My point in telling this story is: we change. And we change our minds. Nothing that we think is chiselled on a stone tablet like something out of *The Flintstones*. Yes, it still floats around on the Internet, some of our bad work, some of our untrue work, or some pieces that we look back on and genuinely wish we'd never written. We don't stay the same, especially during our formative years. Hell, I will be a different person *again* in ten years' time, or even tomorrow. I have come to terms with the fact that I did not know what I know now when I wrote that piece. In my mind, that's *not me* any more.

If you have ever done something you regret too, if you have ever inadvertently been a troll yourself, remember this: human beings have the power to change, to move on from their past or some stupid thing they wrote. You can. And you will. It doesn't matter if no one else has – all that matters is that you have moved on and forgiven yourself. You had a learning moment, now move on. People often find it embarrassing to change their mind, but I think it's healthy to admit it when you want to change direction.

For me the Internet has always been a blissful means of connecting and communicating with like-minded individuals. Every day I stumble across something that adds a spark, big or small, to my everyday life. A song, a joke, a new book recommendation, a column or a blog post that makes me pause and look out of the window for a few minutes, in a little bubble of thought. But what happens when the same Wifi connection that brings you hundreds of inspiring conversations suddenly turns sour? What if, above your laptop, black clouds start to hover over your happy den, like J. K. Rowling's famous Dementors, sucking away at your optimistic and rainbow-coloured lens on the world and shitting all over your parade? What if people start *hating* you from behind their laptops? What if your definition of yourself soon becomes muddled by what other people, who you don't know, think of you?

'You can't hate me!' I whisper quietly, inside. 'I'm a nice person! I like everybody!'

Lesson number one in the Land of the Internet: no one is safe. Who cares if you think you're a nice person? If you have a voice on the Internet you will get shit thrown at you. And what makes you more likely to have shit thrown at you? If you are a young woman with an opinion.

As a young wannabe writer following my favourite famous writers online, one thing I was never braced for was the sheer amount of horrific abuse you get piled on you if you express your opinions on the Internet. As someone who has always thought other people's lives were perfect, without any negativity, it is important for me to share this with other writers who are just starting out. It's not all rainbows and butterflies. And it's not easy putting yourself out there. The fact is that sometimes I want to switch it off altogether when things get tricky. But who am I kidding? I've made it my life's work to overshare and sometimes I don't feel it's a conscious choice: writing to me is like a mix between breathing and therapy. Therapy with typos. The question is: what do you care about more? Writing and having a voice, or having to overcome some very sour comments?

Because it's unavoidable: some people will always have a bone to pick with you. They'll make something up or they'll say something so agonisingly true that you'll be forced to actually believe it yourself. Having a platform means having an audience but that audience will never be 100 per cent in favour of you. Some comments are easy to brush off and laugh about with your friends. *Some* are. But I'm talking about the ones that sting. On articles, on blog posts, on Twitter, on Facebook, on forums, on websites. The ones that really hurt. The ones where people outwardly let you know they hate your work. The venom that swirls around behind your back. Passive-aggressive behaviour. Anonymous haters. This is part and parcel of being a young writer/journalist. I do expect it. I've grown up with it.

You are not what people say about you, but what you reply to. Meaning: if you don't reply or give them airtime, they haven't won, and they haven't got what they want from you.

There's a horrible place on the Internet which is a forum dedicated to hating on popular lifestyle bloggers on the web. The forum houses hundreds of users who just go on there to pick out things they don't like from these blogs. Ironically, they are giving these blogs traffic and the people contributing are probably their most loyal fans because they seem to go onto the blogs every day. The insults will range from 'that Instagram selfie she posted is so arrogant' to 'where does she get all her money from? She must just be rich' to 'I bet she knows someone in the industry' to 'she obviously got all of that on a plate'. See, I don't buy all that negativity. Because the people they are insulting are getting off their arses each morning and creating something they love. They are documenting their lives in the way they want. It makes absolutely no difference to them if these forum-dwellers don't like it.

When I interviewed the incredibly talented Grace Helbig, YouTuber, TV presenter and all-round Internet wonder woman, I asked her about how she deals with negativity and trolls:

'It's so insanely hard to completely ignore it and I would say next to impossible. Our brains remember pain so much easier than nice things. I have to laugh at them because it takes so much extra energy to be a negative person than a positive one. And also – why? Life is so hard and complicated for all of us, why try and make it more complicated?'

We chatted about how someone might leave a really long, mean YouTube comment, and how if that energy were channelled differently then it could have been used for that person to write their own blog post or short story or a nice email to a friend. Everything you write down is energy: commenting negatively on someone else's creation is just a waste of time.

I'm not a 'yeah, whatever!' person. Sometimes I really struggle to digest unpleasant feedback and I will think about a specific dig made at me for weeks on end. I'll be going about my regular day and bouncing along happily and then boom: I'll hear that comment in my ear. Give me 500 nice comments and I will remember the one that hates me. Like in Baz Luhrmann's spoken-word hit

'Everybody's Free (to Wear Sunscreen)' this one line resonated with me: 'Remember compliments you receive. Forget the insults. If you succeed in doing this, tell me how.'

I now feel like I have the power to turn those insults into a positive learning experience. That's not to say I don't wallow first. But I'm also not a victim: my life is great and I'm the sort of person who will take a shit situation, call a friend and buy a crisp glass of white wine for us both and talk it out until it's not even a silver lining any more, it's a huge glittering silver cloud. There are friends I have around me who make me feel bulletproof. Often I think that's my biggest achievement. My tribe.

But it has taken a while to reach this point.

Life is short and I don't want to spend any of it being angry. Some people will never like me, even if I swing by their house with a hamper of Lindt chocolate bunnies, because they already have a perception of me that is totally out of my control. It's like me trying to change the direction of a car using only my mind. But that's okay, I don't need to go to Lucky Voice Karaoke and drink a bottle of red wine with everyone on the Internet. The important thing is I have a healthy relationship with myself and take advice from those who I love, and that simple equation means I'll always be happy with what I've got.

I've also learned, which is perhaps a contradiction, that I won't play it safe. If I 'bring on' any animosity then I will respect others but I won't apologise for my opinions. I will always say what I think. I will always be honest. And I will ALWAYS be open to a two-way conversation. I don't want 'haters' but I do want peers who challenge me and readers who healthily disagree with me.

If you make something and put it out there into the world, you will always get feedback whether it's healthy criticism or unnecessary spitefulness. Being a woman with opinions comes with backlash occasionally. It would be so much easier to live behind the scenes and never to venture front of stage. But the pockets of negativity that float around the web aren't going to go away anytime soon so now's the time to learn to deal with it. Time to be firm about your own reality.

Own your story. Never be silenced.

'So what if we repeat the same themes? So what if we circle around the same ideas, again and again, generation after generation?'

Liz Gilbert, Big Magic

chapter 12
Anonymous Was a Woman

1998

My school teacher, Mr Williams, bounced up and down, wearing only socks on his feet on the sports-hall floor.

'Simon says turn around. Simon says touch your toes! Simon says sit on the floor!'

We all do as we're told.

'Touch your head!'

A few children get called out and have to go and sit on the benches along the wall, looking glum.

'Bad luck, darlings! I didn't say Simon says!'

The teacher, beaming, was clearly enjoying the game as much as everyone else was.

I sidled up to the teacher at the front of the class.

'Why do we have to do what Simon says? I don't know Simon.'

'It's only a *game*, Emma.'

'I know. But I don't want to listen to a man I don't know.'

2014

I sat down in the audience at a panel event at Sutton House in Homerton with sweaty palms. It was early 2014, and the event was called 'What Do We Tell Our Daughters?' I attended it with a friend from the year below me at university called Clare. We'd rekindled our friendship (which means we found each other on Twitter) two years after I graduated, realising just how many feminist opinions we both had in common.

Clare was part of the feminist society at Southampton University, which I'd avoided in favour of going on sunbeds and having sex with men who treated me badly. (Case in point: the guy who didn't believe me when I said I thought I'd broken my wrist and persuaded me to have sex with him anyway. Turned out I had sprained it badly. My friend had to drive me to A&E the next morning in the previous night's clothes.) Basically Clare was off being a radical feminist in the making and doing amazing things to help others. While I was busy degrading myself in every possible way, Clare was knee-deep in activism and banner-waving, launching campaigns and doing good deeds all around the university campus.

It took me a few more years before I discovered feminism myself and started collecting empowering women around me, and thank God I did. Finding feminism and feminist heroes I could identify with saved me from being a bad version of myself, with streaky tan lines and self-esteem the size of a red ant. Instead of feeling down whenever I was the butt of a sexist joke, I'd have the newfound energy to take people on. Instead of responding with nervous laughter, I'd think *fuck YOU!* We give birth! We have twice as many nerve endings on our clitorises than men do on their penises! We do everything you already do! We grow miniature humans in our bellies and can still function at work normally while sharing our organs and water and food supplies with another small human! WHAT CAN YOU DO?

I overheard many different points of view around me during the event. Some of which were: 'People who get feminist and feminine mixed up need to get in the sea' and 'I simply cannot talk to anyone who hasn't read *Bad Feminist*' and 'Why the fuck is Rupert Murdoch tweeting again?' and 'Feminism doesn't mean I have to like all women. I really hate a lot of women' and 'Did you know that Sarah Jessica Parker apparently doesn't believe in feminism?'

It was a lot to take in. The truth was, it all made me nervous because I wasn't one of those people who had a solid opinion on everything. *In your twenties you are meant to be working things out.* (I still am. I probably still will be when I'm sixty.) Everyone was ranting. I was treading water, trying to stay above it all, attempting to be in the conversation but certainly not wanting to be leading any of it. I didn't know what I thought, yet. I just wanted equality like everyone else, and felt totally uneducated about all the different nuances and terminologies of feminism. The Internet was exactly that thing. The thing to educate me. I would make sure I had a mix of voices in my timeline.

But due to the explosion of blogs, Twitter and forums, we all have the free tools to tell the world exactly what we think, whenever we want. However, the negative side of this is that our own idea of feminism might not align with other online communities and means we are at risk of being scolded for our beliefs. Due to the existence of social variables – small niche groups, media influences, living situations, privilege, diverse cultural groups and ever-changing political factors – the definition of feminism will of course mean something different from woman to woman, person to person. But surely it shouldn't have to be this complicated. Surely we can all agree on the next steps for the feminist agenda, together? The amount of time people spend slating each other on Twitter on this subject is slightly worrying, mainly because doing *anything* else, other than that, would be better for moving the conversation forward. Spending sunny afternoons indoors having a Twitter spat is literally the worst use of anyone's time. Trolls clearly aren't frequenting any comedy nights or going out dancing enough. Arguing online achieves nothing because no one ever wins. It stunts the movement. It's not good for us. A big debate with someone in person or as group might have results, but spitting insults in 140 characters? It's pointless.

At the end of the event, Clare and some other girls went off for a drink with the panellists but I decided to head for home, exhausted from the week and feeling like I could do with an early night, however much it meant I would be missing out on some brilliant late-night networking.

I said my goodbyes then decided to pop back into the venue, as I was bursting for a wee. I headed for the loo and waited behind the door for it to become free. A woman with very bright yellow Crocs appeared next to me, her eyes piercing the side of my face. Out of the corner of my eye I could see she was leaning slightly towards me and I felt she was about to engage, although I was unsure what it could possibly be about: was she before me in the queue? Did I just push in? Did I have loo roll on my shoe? Was she about to out herself as my long-lost relative? I was pondering all of this while my face was buried in my phone, aggressively favouriting tweets.

I heard her clearing her throat.

'On your phones – you kids are on your phones all the time!'

She had a scratchy voice. I gave a little smile and awkwardly moved my feet.

'The Internet. It does *nothing* for female empowerment really, does it?'

I turned around to check she was talking to me. She didn't have an unfriendly face, but it did look very old. She leaned against the wall, playing with a large chunky ring on her finger.

'If you ask me, it does nothing. It highlights the very worst of society, and the worst of human nature. The very worst. Women still aren't listened to. The Internet won't help.'

She was glancing down at my phone and shaking her head when she saw how many apps I was obsessively opening and re-opening.

'You won't make any change in the world on that … thing.' She gestured towards my iPhone.

I realised I was too scared to argue. I knew I didn't agree. Sure, the way we communicate now has changed dramatically over the last decade, but it didn't mean the Internet hadn't brought *some* good with it. However, my late grandma on my mum's side, who taught me her impeccable table manners with a no-bullshit attitude, had instructed me to respect my elders, so this what I was did. I just nodded, swallowed and bit my tongue and put my grubby iPhone back into my pocket, pretending to agree with her.

She asked me what I did, and I told her I was a writer and worked in social media. She looked colourful, with her bright yellow shoes, thick-framed glasses, a woollen hat and a bright orange notepad. She wearing a badge that said 'Don't Ask My Husband, Ask Me'. Maybe she had it all figured it out. Maybe my Internet addiction was a bad thing. Maybe I was becoming distracted from things I could actually get involved with, physically, in person.

'In my day – and I'm nearly eighty-five years old – you'd take to the streets if you had a problem. Not just flippantly share an opinion here and there online. Does nothing. Hashtag this. Hashtag that. People are just harping on and on and on. Nothing gets *solved*. You don't *need* all these irrelevant individual opinions floating around. People need to form groups and meet up in person, go out there ...' She exhaled loudly.

The toilet cubicle suddenly swung open and became free. I wanted to respond to her but I was close to urinating down the side of my leg. I apologised coyly and went into the toilet, locking the loo door. She could probably hear me pee.

As I sat on the loo, mid-wee, it occurred to me she wouldn't have taken me seriously if she knew I'd used the time sitting on the toilet to retweet some quotes from Oprah's Twitter feed.

I had to come up with a response as to whether my addiction to the Internet could serve some sort of purpose and help me be a better woman. I decided that even if Twitter wasn't overly helpful in furthering the feminist movement overall (which I thought it had), it was at least furthering MY own voice, and all I wanted to do was encourage others to share theirs. I was learning. And learning, more importantly, about those around me, and those in other parts of the world. My friend Laura calls those times you realise you fucked up 'learning moments'. When you tweet or blog something that is socially not cool, you can say, 'Hey, you guys, I'm having a learning moment.' And equally: 'I know I can't have too many learning moments, I'm trying my best but feel free to hate me if I fuck things up too many times in a row.'

I psyched myself up to respond to her. When I came out of the toilet, though, she'd disappeared. I suppose this next part of the chapter is my response to her, the lady with no name in the loo. This is my explanation of why I believe the Internet has facilitated brilliant movements and empowered many women.

Although it brings with it a host of shaming, the Internet also brings tools to help women stand against and eliminate their shame. Having a blog, or an online channel that is yours, means that you will always have a voice; a voice to speak against the bullshit of life. People in the public arena can now take on the mainstream media or the gossip websites whose only goal is to shame people. A few decades ago, there would be nothing they could do, but now the celebrity can speak on their own social media platform and take back control. Anyone can hit 'publish' on their own version of their story.

I realised that my Internet fetish is finding strong women with unique voices and asking them to be my friend. I did not need to look far to find examples of women who use the Internet to amplify their ideas. Thanks to my blog, I feel I have a community of like-minded women surrounding me. But there's always room at the inn and I'll never be that person who says 'I have enough friends, thanks'.

I found people who made me feel less alone. Represented. Safety in numbers. I hope every woman finds a group of people who represent them. And I hope we will reach a time when we see that same representation in all other cultural media, such as film or TV. We need to see ourselves reflected back to us. All of us.

I don't think it's a coincidence that the same year I discovered the books and films of women who reflected who I wanted to be, I began to find myself. Culture and art help us find our buried souls, the feelings that have been squashed by social pressures, tradition and engrained stereotypes. I'd take cuttings from magazines about paintings, films and books and apply them to my own life. The little pieces would map out who I'd want to be. I'd treasure these imperfect creations by imperfect women.

Growing up, I didn't connect with many of the women presented to me on TV during my teens, like Kelly Kapowski from *Saved by the Bell* and Britney Spears in *Crossroads*. They all had fabulous stomachs and looked insane in a crop top. But then, in my twenties, women like Amy Schumer and Mindy Kaling came bowling in and openly commented on the bullshit culture of women having to Look A Certain Way all the damn time. On a recent *SNL* sketch, Amy said: 'We have to be a role model for these little girls, because who do they have? All they have really is the Kardashians.' I mean, I don't mind the Kardashians, but constantly being told how to contour my face wasn't helping me feel better about myself. I read Rebecca Solnit's *Men Explain Things to Me*. I made an eighty-year-old feminist pen pal, the author Leah Fritz, by accident. I reviewed her book *Thinking Like a Woman* (published in 1975) after I found it in a second-hand bookshop on Charing Cross Road. Leah then found my blog post that mentioned the book. 'I Google myself from time to time,' she said in an email, 'and I think we are kindred spirits.' I followed opinionated women on Twitter. My role models had changed.

I came across a quote on Pinterest that made me pause for thought. In all seriousness, it actually made me feel terribly sad: 'For most of history, "anonymous" was a woman.' Think of how many 'anonymous' works there are in the literary canon. Thousands. It would make sense for women to hide behind a man's name or 'anon' when they were living in a world in which their voices were suppressed. And that applies to this day, too. Why couldn't J. K. Rowling have been straight up Joanne on the cover?

Despite the modern-day belief that we should be encouraged to raise our voices, there's a horrible irony that when women do 'speak up', we often get scolded it for it. There are countless examples of famous women who bravely speak up on a matter, be it political or personal, get applauded, and then get torn down. There was a recent article on the parody website The Onion that summed this up well: 'Girl Finally Speaking Up Enough For People To Critique Her Speaking Voice'. Jo Freeman coined this practice as 'trashing' in a piece she wrote in 1976 for *Ms* magazine.

I recently scribbled down, with a lump in my throat, a quote by Jane Fonda during an interview with Amanda de Cadenet: 'At puberty, the majority of girls, their voices go underground. They don't disappear. They go underground. That's why girls are the agents of change, because you don't have to scratch too deep to say, "Hey, remember how you used to be?"'

I noticed it with me and my friends. Before puberty, we wouldn't be afraid to tell people exactly what we thought of them. We would stretch our hands up high in the classroom if someone asked us a question and we would fight over the 'C' bib in the netball squad. We all wanted to be centre. Centre of attention. Centre of our own worlds. We'd cover ourselves with bright feather boas and dance into any room with no insecurities. We wouldn't even look in the mirror. In my after-school drama club I would audition for any part under the sun, even if it included a solo, and I couldn't even sing. My confidence was a sort of naivety: I was immune to negative feelings because I didn't know enough about the world yet. I wasn't aware of my physique either.

How things change. I would never in a million years stand on a stage and sing now. Although the thought of live singing is terrifying, pathetically it's more to do with the fact that the people in the front row seats would get a bad angle of my body.

I suppose you could say the school I attended was a feminist school. Everywhere we looked there were extremely strong women in positions of authority, leading us by example. It was an all-girls, pep-talking, confidence-growing powerhouse of a school. It was drummed into each and every one of us, every day, that we would 'be successful', but the definitions of success were left broad enough for us not to feel pigeon-holed. We were all permanently high on the idea of succeeding, which was great but also slightly intense. It meant different things to different people. We were, of course, extremely lucky to be surrounded with such optimism. On the last day of A levels, we huddled into a room and received a stern talking-to, by one of our tutors:

'When you get out there in the big wide world, girls, grab the bull by its horns! Spread your wings! Go, go! Make your mark on the world, and don't take no for an answer!'

I don't really remember a competitive atmosphere at the time because everyone in the class was so different. There were the musical geniuses, the wannabe astronauts, the sporty girls who would play for the country, the doctors, the theatrical talents, the hardcore academics who would go on to do PhDs, and the people who really didn't give a flying fuck where they ended up. We were lucky because we were given the tools to shout as loudly as we could. The world really was our oyster. Our teachers made us feel invincible. The motto of our school was 'Where girls come first'. Snigger.

But despite this cheerleading atmosphere all around us, something started to change in us girls as soon as we hit puberty. As we started approaching our early teens, grew boobs and cheekbones and got our first agonising periods, we noticeably, as a collective, became quieter. I would sit politely and cover my mouth when I laughed. I covered my face with my hair. I was embarrassed to run during sports. My boobs felt ridiculous when I ran and I felt ashamed of my body. I'd look in the mirror and hate the curve of my hips. I grew conscious of the hair on my body. We'd worry that our private thoughts might be embarrassing, just like our bodies, so we became more invisible. It seems that, more often than not, girls going through puberty accidentally get hold of Harry Potter's invisibility cloak. My personality and voice retired to the basement and took a while to crawl back out.

When we talk about 'female voices' in the world, it's hard to deny that there is lack of them, not just during our teenage years, but in general – in literature, films, books, or in big political or financial decisions. Women's voices are so often told to go back underground. We only have to remember the story of Monica Lewinsky to see just how easy it is for women to be shamed. Her voice subsequently went underground for a whole decade. Women have been shamed for *simply being women* for hundreds of thousands of years.

During my teenage years, before I found the word 'feminism', I knew I was treated differently for being a girl, even if it was the smallest thing, like being told off for not being 'lady-like' or being cat-called even at the school gates. My mind was full of so many things, trying to make sense of it all, all whirring around in my teenage brain. I was shocked every time I read more depressing statistics of how so many women in Third World countries were illiterate compared to men. By the fact that men would make up the majority of funny comedians on shows like *Live at the Apollo* or any mainstream comedy panel. That politicians' voices were mainly male. That only male sports teams received media coverage. That most of my school friends had dads who made the decisions over the mothers and had the main bread-winning career. Inequality was visible everywhere.

It would be impossible to write a book about growing up online without mentioning feminism. For the first time in history, we can hear an equal share of female voices in the world. And the Internet has enabled this. The Internet has allowed anyone and everyone to shout as loud as they want to, and have a place to channel their thoughts, hopes and dreams, for anyone to come across it. The Internet has allowed this change, and it's also put a spotlight on huge stagnant issues too. It feels powerful to be surrounded by young women who have blogs that talk about abortion, sex, health, periods, rape, relationships, love, depression, mental health, motherhood, embarrassment, worry, stress, racism and careers. We are living in a time where we have voices and people are listening. Loud, deep, clear and honest voices of women of different races, sexual orientation and class. The Internet has allowed us to have a space, to debate, talk, open up, share and connect. To work towards taking up half the space that is rightfully ours. It has given us a place to practise speaking again. To find the voice we always had, that went into hiding all those years back.

One of the reasons my blog meant so much to me personally was because it was my small act of saying: 'I will not be silenced, this is my voice.' It is important for *everyone to have a voice*. Whether you are fighting against female genital mutilation, or you want to close the pay gap at corporate firms, or you are railing against the fact that #EverydaySexism exists in the environment in which you live. The world is big, and everyone's problems are different in scale. But every problem is still worth voicing. We are not there yet. There is still raging inequality. But social media has created a new kind of democracy and *that* is exciting.

I didn't start the blog just because I wanted to speak myself. Being a woman with a voice is not just about you. I learned that you cannot speak on other people's behalf, but you can share your own truth and listen to other people's. Because there are a lot of young women out there who need to be listened to. Statistics from Girlguiding show that almost half (46 per cent) of girls aged seventeen to twenty-one have personally needed help with their mental health and nearly three in five girls aged eleven to twenty-one say that mental health is awkward to talk about. Girls are so busy feeling ashamed about so many 'girl' things that their voices remain mute.

But the response to raising your voice on the Internet can be something that none of us is prepared for. I certainly was not taught at school how *mean* people can be behind the safety of their keyboards. Or how certain 'groups' can target and try and silence a woman speaking her mind. Especially on Twitter. Ever since Ricky Gervais said, 'Twitter is just people shouting into a bin', I do try to be light-hearted about things. But scary threats on Twitter have driven female journalists offline for daring to have a voice. It can still be confusing, navigating one space with lots of different opinions all trying to dominate it. And if you're still forming those opinions, it can be a rough sea to float across, and you will get dragged under occasionally, too.

I could see where the lady in the loo was coming from, that she didn't seem to understand why anyone would listen to any old random with a Twitter account. Once upon a time there were only three places to consume media: radio, TV and newspapers. Now it is endlessly flowing towards us on our phones. We forget this is still new in the grand scheme of the world. Angry think-pieces, tweets, articles, ideas and opinions are directly accessed via our eyeballs every time we log into our social media newsfeeds and if we're not careful they can seep into our brains every minute of every day. On average I normally have around fifteen tabs open on Google Chrome – all things I feel I should read to better myself. This is my daily cycle of Internet consumption. Highs met with lows. But how can we be sure of what's important, and what's worth listening to, when everyone is shouting all at once?

I realise that with all this over-stimulation, maybe, just maybe, the Internet is fucking me up a bit. It reminds me of school – all the subtle digs in the form of sub-tweets, straight-up bullying, and instances when people try to make others feel intellectually inferior by using obscure buzzwords. Little 140-character capsules fly into my brain at a rapid pace, often leaving me totally overwhelmed. It's hard to navigate through the noise. Maybe Loo Lady was right that *most* stuff on the Internet is time-wasting garbage. I don't want to see most of it. Reading twenty-five different opinions on whether a celebrity should or shouldn't wear heels when pregnant isn't really necessary for my personal growth. But I can't be stopped; I cannot get myself off the ride. To fight Internet Overwhelm I sometimes have to turn my phone onto airplane mode while I sleep. This is what we have to do now: we have to tell our phones to GO AWAY while we sleep so that our brains can have a break from heat radiation, just for a few short hours.

I guess I'm kind of envious that Loo Lady doesn't believe in getting involved in the Internet nonsense. I often do feel a little enslaved to it. I'm obsessed with being up to date with what's #trending, what's 'cool', what's CATEGORICALLY NOT ON and which of the new sexy social networks (called something like Snaggle or Flappn where you can meet the man of your dreams in your dreams, via in-built brain technology, for example) is worth my time and app space. Scrolling and wading through hundreds of pieces of news is my full-time job, literally. I am a plugged-in, all-consuming, twenty-six-year-old, technology-obsessed fiend. My thumbs spend the majority of their day tapping and scrolling on my iPhone and iPad and my little laptop hanging out of my handbag. So hell knows how anyone else can keep up with the tsunami of daily new information if I'm struggling and my actual JOB is to endlessly scroll on Twitter every day. I'm a professional scroller, and I am beginning to slowly, slowly lose my mind. One of the reasons the Internet has started to scare me is because I am becoming apathetic. I am shrugging so much off because there's so much to take in. I get angry, and then get apathetic. This is not a good thing. I often feel the constant need for people to practise one-upmanship on an issue is getting in the way of moving forward. The way in which feminism is presented on the Internet can be complex and intimidating. I studied feminism at school, writing Mary Wollstonecraft quotes in my diary and being all 'hell yeah, I am a feminist, OBVIOUSLY!!!' But then I encountered Online Feminism. It is a whole new world. There are layers. There are groups. There are trolls. There is what Jenni Konner describes as 'snark'. There are a million different 'types' of feminism. 'Lipstick feminism', 'cupcake feminism', 'white feminism', 'TMI (oversharing) feminism', 'radical feminism',

'BlackBerry feminism', or one I made up: 'you-can't-sit-with-us feminism'.

The finger-pointing reminded me of some forums I'd come across regarding parenting, which I had researched for a feature. Those forums get *nasty*. People don't hesitate in pointing out what you're doing wrong and why. 'I can't believe she still breastfeeds!' or 'You should never ever let them watch more than two hours of TV!' or 'She went back to work too early, the kid will have insecurity issues for life!' Quite frankly, it quickly filled me with fear about having babies, which is a shame.

Instead of encouraging us to form a sisterhood, it often feels like things are going the other way on the Internet. Every day you could give yourself a migraine from all the arguments about feminism, which, ironically, isn't exactly moving us forward in the right direction. It's like a bunch of people arguing while dangling off the edge of a cliff, without clubbing together to find a practical solution on how to get down it safely. As Caitlin Moran put it: 'Ultimately, when feminism has won, feminism will disappear.' I don't understand how fighting with other women on the Internet will solve our problems so, sadly, I have decided often to just 'dip out' of the conversation, and leave everyone else fighting as if they're in a grand, action-packed battle scene out of *The Hobbit*. PEOPLE ARE SCARED TO GET IT WRONG because they might get attacked by someone with a virtual sword on a virtual horse. It's the slippery banana skin beneath people's feet.

Because if we're still trying to reach the equality nirvana, we're not going to get very far if we're all busy bullying each other.

*

Of course, there isn't an official 'Internet Police'. This means that users take it on themselves to decide what should be censored and what shouldn't. There are certain barriers put in place by the Twitter Gods, to make sure that nothing really *awful* happens (which of course it still does, but the aim is just that there be less of it). If someone threatens to bomb your house via a tweet then that person will be suspended if enough people report it. And lower down the Internet-crime scale, it is now Twitter Illegal to steal jokes: *Big Brother is watching you* and can now detect (rather cleverly) if you have ripped off someone's hilarious joke and posted it as your own. (To be very honest, I'm glad this rule has only just come into play because I stole someone's joke once and I don't regret it at all. I was drowning in retweets.)

Other than that, you're on your own, and inevitably this means that there are times you find yourself facing the Internet 'snark' alone. But that's not the main reason I've got beef with the overwhelming nature of social media these days. The reason I am exasperated is because we are also in the middle of a rise in Internet Outrage Culture. I don't think this is good for creativity, or any type of art or debate. Anything can get shot down within seconds via gangs of virtual bullies. Anything you say can be picked apart, twisted and turned to make you a Bad Guy even if deep down you really don't think you're the culprit. For example, right now, as I type this chapter, I stumbled across a celebrity story about how a Hollywood actress is 'wrong' for not breastfeeding her kid; one of my favourite male authors is being ripped apart for saying he wants to write a book about masculinity, with eye-rolling comments coming in thick and fast ('Sure that's what the world needs, another book by a MAN'); a female comic is being branded as having a 'blind spot for racism' after some controversial jokes; and a hugely successful female author has had her tweets rounded up on Storify to reveal all the different times she's used offensive slang words in conversations – each tweet has been lifted out of context and grouped together to make her look homophobic. They might all be wrong. They might all be right. Everyone has a right to freedom of speech. Everyone has a right to be offended. But if no one ever offended anyone, no meaty conversations would ever take place.

We are all outraged all the time but that's because we're allowed to be, and for the first time ever, social media (especially Twitter) is allowing us to have a *global conversation* and voice lots of different things we all believe in. And what happens during global conversations? What happens when millions of different people from all walks of life all gather around one big table? Disagreements happen. Big ones, and small ones. Of course they do! And not everyone is involved in the conversations, of course, it's the people who have access to or enjoy using Twitter. That's a certain type of person too – one that enjoys tweeting their thoughts, opinions and what they had for breakfast. I know plenty of people who would never want to do a tweet in their life. They can't be arsed with the drama.

The world is far from perfect. If we think about how much stuff there is still to fix, it can be incredibly depressing.

The main issue that is being fought out on Twitter each day is priority. The priority of problems. Everyone has an issue close to their heart. As a white Westerner, I am aware that my problems are not as important or serious as those elsewhere. Yet, I feel it is important for every human to have a way of telling their story. Many people feel like it is a waste of breath to even air your grievances if you live in the UK because *we've got it good*, but silencing smaller problems isn't the answer either. We can stand up for ourselves if we don't want to shave our armpits (however petty that seems in the grand scheme of the world) but we can *also* join movements that will help our sisters in other countries.

It's messy and complicated out there, and some days it's hard to go on Twitter and face up to the issues other people face. We're learning how to wrap armour around ourselves every time we go online and have an opinion because of the backlash and anger towards people with differing opinions to us. Jon Ronson, in his 2015 book *So You've Been Publicly Shamed*, describes this brand new world as a place 'where the smartest way to survive is to be bland'. Becoming afraid of your voice being heard would bring us right back to square one. Being bland doesn't change the world.

Conversations regarding feminism are often so academic they risk alienating a lot of women. I find myself being more scared of women's opinions of me on the Internet than men. I dress for women's compliments, not men's. I love women. I'm more obsessed with other women than anything else but, my God: girls know how to hurt you with words.

Jessica Grose, who works on Lena Dunham's Lenny Letter, describes it as this: 'The Internet Feminism conversation can be very circular and limiting and exclusive,' she said. 'And it saddens me to see that a lot of the competition is about saying "you're not feminist enough": trying to kick people out of feminism rather than bring them in.'

This is exactly how I've been feeling for years now. I never feel enough. Even in a movement like feminism, fighting for the equality of sexes, I still don't feel like I ever get it completely right. Shouty people become more popular on the Internet because they threaten and scare people by writing in capital letters or sneering at someone in a sub-tweet. You could just get on that bandwagon too and yell 'WITCH! WITCH!' if you want. It is easier to follow a crowd, and many group opinions are formed in a domino effect, one spurring on the other. Our newsfeeds of millions of thoughts turns into a maze and you can either choose to follow someone down their path or you can brave your own, carving out your own opinions and forming your own online identity. If you have *all the answers in the world*, then go forth! I'm jealous! That means the Internet will never get you down! P.S. Are you a human?

There are lots of things to complain about regarding social media: the way the news is spread, the way people joke too early when a celebrity dies, the way cliques so easily form (from school friends to middle-aged journalists), and the way the silliest tweet can put you in a bad mood. The humble-brags and the real brags. Big issues, small issues. It appears people like making lists of people that they Love, Hate to Love, Love to Hate, Hate-Follow, Feel Indifferent About; the They're-OK-Actuallys and Not Decided on Yet.

But there are so many good things too. The Internet allows everyone a voice and a platform. Social media and blogging gave me a voice, which led to this book. It's not about being right, or the best, or the loudest. It's about being brave enough to show up, despite criticism and anxiety. Being a woman and voicing your opinion is always a feminist act in my opinion.

No one can ignore big online movements now. This is vastly different from the days of pre-Internet newspapers, which just said in tiny print: 'Send us a letter!' Of course, this was actually code for: 'Write us a letter and we will laugh at it before we set fire to it, ha ha ha! It'll never see the light of day, suckers!' Instead of writing a letter to a PO box number, which would never be read, anyone can leave a comment for the world to see, and rightly so. Any 'unknown person' can have five minutes of fame or the potential for their opinion to go 'viral'. Traditional newspaper columnists don't have the same level of clout anymore. As Internet users we have to navigate through messages of hate, just as frequently as we have to navigate through thousands of Instagram accounts dedicated to really good quotes, normally written in Comic Sans, badly Photoshopped onto a stock photo of a rice field. There's a lot of positive and negative 'content' out there, and as young and impressionable millennials, part of our job is to digest it, decipher it, and work out Who The Fuck We Are.

What makes our generation different from those previous is that we can have an idea and then actually spread that idea to thousands via a social media strategy of some kind. I spoke to Nathalie Gordon, one of the brains behind the #ThisDoesntMeanYes campaign. The project was launched in conjunction with Rape Crisis South London to raise awareness that such things as a short skirt, a low-cut top or a red lip is not an invitation for a man to take what he chooses. Social media was at the heart of the idea; Gordon admitted to basing the whole campaign around a hashtag, which is how it took off: 'One of the things I have 100 per cent taken from this – the coldest learning – is that no message, no matter what it is, will be successful if you cannot condense it into a tweet or even better, a hashtag.' We are living in a Hashtag world and a message does need to be condensed; perhaps it is our shortened attention spans, but equally it is the fact that we are fighting against thousands of other things in people's newsfeeds, and so we have about two seconds to capture someone's attention. Another reason the campaign was successful is because the founders shared the campaign manifesto on Instagram; Nathalie explained that as it was 'sharable content that had a message that people wanted to share for themselves, that did a lot of the hard work for us'. That's the thing: people see a message that aligns with their beliefs and therefore will post an image or quote on their social feeds without much prompting. I asked her which online movements she was inspired by: '#HeForShe, #EverydaySexism, Bodyform "The Truth", #LikeAGirl, Black Lives Matter, #IllRideWithYou, #BringBackOurGirls ... the list is endless. I'm inspired by it all. I'm inspired by the masses and how much power there is in group thought and the combined forces of those who care.'

In a world where periods are still 'gross' and never mentioned in mainstream films or TV shows, we can talk to social media to spread the love (and blood). Recently women all around the world were dangling tampons from their mouths to rid the taboo about these fluffy little pieces of cotton that we put up our vaginas, and using the hashtag #justatampon. There were YouTube parodies of Taylor Swift's 'Bad Blood' that focused on the intricacies of using tampons.

And these aren't the only groundbreaking campaigns that have recently gained popularity online. #AskHerMore was all about asking women more questions on the red carpet (complemented by Amy Schumer's campaign to #AskHimLess). The movement behind #YouOKSis challenged street harassment. #SayHerName was to make sure the world was aware just how much police brutality affects black women. #LoveYourLines was a celebration for women to show off their stretch marks. The hashtag #GrowingUpAGirl saw an outpouring of messages from girls describing things that made them feel embarrassed growing up: hiding tampons from male teachers or being told they couldn't climb trees because it wasn't 'ladylike'. The Malala fund started #WeAreSilent, raising awareness of the millions of girls who have been denied the basic right of going to school. Laura Bates's #EverydaySexism movement made thousands and thousands of women feel less alone, and showed the world that sexism still happens every minute of every day. #FreeTheNipple called for woman to reclaim their bodies. The #NotBuyingIt campaign was started by the Representation Project to shine a light on adverts aimed at women that objectify and stereotype us. It might just be a hashtag, but it's better than nothing. According to data from Twitter, stated in an article from 2014 called 'Hashtag Feminism': 'conversation about "feminism" has increased by 300 per cent on the platform over the past three years.' A quick search on Instagram shows me there are over 1 million photos shared with #feminism in the caption.

The elderly woman next to me in the toilets had a point. Perhaps we are running the risk of talking the talk without actually involving ourselves in real politics behind the campaigns we happily retweet. We need to get out into the world and *do more*. Hashtags aren't always the *answer*. But, like defending a bad boyfriend, I have to stick up for the Internet, no matter how awful it can be, at times. It's done a lot for us, to help us find the voices and outspoken communities that have been denied us for so many centuries. This isn't a phase: we will continue to use the Internet to build communities, campaign and make change.

'That's what we do now. We grieve online as much as we do in person.'

Michael Reilly, technologyreview.com, 2016

chapter 13
Death in the Digital Age

2016

The Internet is guilty of perpetuating shallow connections. A 'like' here, a 'poke' there, or a secret stalking session without the person in question knowing you are thinking of them. Here's a scary thought: if you didn't go online for a few days, would anyone *really* notice? Perhaps you'd get a few texts and calls from your family, close friends or partner perhaps, but outside of that, would all your (on average) 150 Facebook 'friends' realise you'd slipped away for a while? Would they call you up asking why you had not posted any selfies lately? Would they notice a you-shaped hole in their newsfeed? If you just went mute, sidling out of the Internet's back door for a few days, would anyone *panic*?

Of course, we'd like to think so. But it's sad to admit that our social newsfeeds are busy and it's hard to keep tabs on all the people who drift in and out of our lives. A friend of mine from school who I see about three times a year, a friend but not a *close* friend, deleted her Facebook page and it took me three months to notice. I realised after something reminded me of her and I searched her name to share a private joke. I didn't know where the hell she was, or where I could get hold of her – I didn't even know where she lived any more. I'd taken our shallow 'connection' on Facebook for granted. We weren't connected, not really.

We take for granted the fact that we can log onto Instagram and see exactly where someone's location is, or see on WhatsApp that a particular person was 'active three minutes ago' to check they are alive and well without actually asking if they are alive and well. When you don't have that information about a friend any more, it makes you realise just how much you rely on it to keep tabs on people. I admit that with friends who I don't see very often, I often check how they're doing on Facebook to ease my concerns or curiosity. It's a scary thought that without a few social networks tying me and my less-close friends together, they would so easily slip away from me. I have to work extra hard at my friendships these days. My friends fall into two camps: two-hour teary FaceTime phone-calls in bed wearing only a bra, or the back-and-forth of half-arsed messages that say 'coffee soon?' followed by a three-month silence.

I don't know half the people on my Facebook, mainly because they're all getting married and have different names now or because we met in the queue for the toilet at a gross house party in 2008 and added each other on Facebook to pass the time, so it takes me about half an hour to realise who someone actually is. I cull people on their birthday because it's the one time I get reminded of them, and think, *who?* I do tend to tweet every five minutes, so I actually reckon my family or boyfriend or boss would think I'd been bru-tally murdered if I hadn't tweeted for an hour. With Wifi even available on long-haul plane journeys now, it is worrying when an active social media user goes quiet.

I 'hid' an old colleague of mine from my Facebook newsfeed a while back and the next time I saw her she was carrying a tiny baby. I'd totally missed the whole pregnancy evolution memo thing. It was a bit of a shock bumping into her in Tesco and awkwardly trying to suss out if the baby was hers, or whether she was going through a career-change involving child daycare. When you're the person posting an update on your huge life milestone, you assume everyone is *paying attention*. They aren't. No one is watching what you are doing. They are refreshing their own profile more times than yours.

If you disappeared from the Internet altogether, could you definitely say you'd be inundated with phone calls? Lucky you, if so. Could you go so far as to say you could survive and keep up lots of friendships without the Internet, full stop? Any computer addict in 2016 needs the Internet to keep in touch with lots of dif-ferent friendship circles. But we're in danger of having hundreds of shallow connections and no deep connections – the sort where someone would scream after two days of silence, 'Where the fuck are you? No kidding!' It's a similar fear I would have when I was a teen, when leaving my Nokia 3210 turned off in a drawer while going on a long holiday. Returning to the drawer, I'd turn the phone on with a bit of tension in my belly. I wouldn't be overly worried that people had been trying to get hold of me; I'd be wor-ried that no one had.

The Internet can also be the place we go to try and get closer to someone from afar. When we miss someone, we scroll through their photos. We type their name into Google. We visit their social media profiles and dip in and out of their life. We try and reach out through a screen. It's the best way of prompting our memories. When my boyfriend is travelling, I look through photo albums of us together. When I'm away from home, I scroll through photos of my family. When someone passes away, a celebrity or a friend, the Internet comes alive with memories. From all corners of the web, we are filled with outpourings of love. Mourning collectively online can make us feel far from alone.

Death has always been on my mind, even as a child. I can't blame it entirely on the Mufasa scene in *The Lion King* but that certainly stayed with me. I had vivid death dreams. I would wake up hot and sticky in bed, thinking my dream was real for a few seconds, then I would cry again, this time with relief when realising it wasn't. I was too aware of people ageing around me. I'd be nervous at the sight of a grey hair on anyone I knew. I'd imagine the worst if someone was running late and I hadn't heard from them. My mind could very easily jump out of control. As I've got older I've tried to use more of the rational side of my brain instead of falling into a pit of anxiety for no real reason.

Now that we spend a large proportion of our lives online, I find myself wondering what happens to all of the 'content' we build up after we die. Because back in the day, if you died you'd just leave your CD collection to a younger family member, or maybe an expensive watch. But now, it's a different story. Now we are tangled up with all sorts of things we own online. We have things we've built up over the years: a funny Twitter feed, a well-optimised Google page, a blog worth a bit of money, perhaps. What about our iTunes collection? A brilliant rating on eBay? A premium Spotify account? The endless photos, videos, pieces of work, online articles? What do we do with all these *things*? Would we want all of our stuff floating around after we've gone? All our memories, available for any Tom, Dick or Harry to access them if they wanted to?

I realised recently that I don't exactly like the way 'memories' are stored online – they often aren't as authentic as physical photos in a box, or simply whatever you remember in your head. Timehop was an app I downloaded and got into a routine of looking at, checking what I'd been doing a year ago, two years ago, five years ago – stalking my own online history. The app would pull in all my old posts from Facebook, Twitter and Instagram. But it started to get me down; I couldn't win because either I'd find myself looking at a great holiday or memory that I wished I could go back to, or I'd be reminded of a friend I no longer talk to because we fell out, or I'd see a selfie of me snogging a past flame, or quite simply a really bad outfit. In short: my own social media history (good and bad) was starting to haunt me and I didn't see the point in bringing up old memories that weren't constructive or helpful to my future. It also reminded me just how much meaningless stuff is buried online. But then I thought: what if our social media history isn't necessarily for us? What if it's just important for us to leave pieces of ourselves behind for other people?

In lots of ways our lives have changed due to the Internet, including how we handle our emotions and privacy in relationships. For example, do we need digital pre-nups in relationships now? In America it's already a thing. If you're planning to get serious with someone and you like sending the odd sexy text now and again (who doesn't?), you can get digital privacy clauses written into your pre-nuptial and post-nuptial documents. Basically it means that any nude photos or emails or nakey screenshots that you sent to your love-rat ex-boyfriend cannot be used in divorce proceedings. I like the sound of this. Take the fucking CD rack by all means, but please don't take my arse pictures and show all your mates down the pub. My arse deserves some respect. Plus the whole point of breaking up is you NEVER GET TO SEE MY BODY AGAIN.

We can even get digital wills puts in place. Facebook has installed a function that allows you to choose an 'heir' who manages your account if you die. (I still have no idea who I'd entrust. You?) What it says on the tin is: 'Choose a legacy contact' for 'your digital afterlife' – imagine that on a billboard as you drive along the M5. Depressing, really. But functional? Futuristic? Maybe. I never really considered it before, but if I really sit down and think about it, yes I do want someone to sort out all my messy online presence after I die. I want good stuff on there. You know what they say: 'If I die, please pick the selfie with the most likes.' Back in 2013, Google similarly allowed people to choose a carer for their digital after-life, but I'm not sure I'd want anyone filing through my emails. However, I would love someone to tinker with my SEO, so that the number one result about me on Google is 'Emma was a GREAT PERSON' and all those hater articles and bad reviews are shifted down to the bottom. You can hide a dead body on the second page of Google, the SEO geeks always say in their presentations.

The Internet has tried to dabble with death in a way that makes me feel uncomfortable. Of course, we are used to such apps as Calorie Counter or FitBit – they help us feel in control of our health and that's fine. Personally I can't think of anything worse that knowing how many calories I've eaten, or confirming how many times I've lifted my right arm in a day, but you know, each to their own. If you enjoy surveillancing your body each day, then good for you! But now we might be going a step too far. In 2004, *Time* magazine reported on an app that 'predicts the date that you're going to die' by using Apple's HealthKit (basically by inputting some light medical history and lifestyle details). Who wants to know that? I categorically *do not* want to know that. But it is interesting to see technology allowing us to discuss death. That is some high-tech shit right there. But it's also really morbid.

As with money, (mainly British) people don't like talking about death openly. Being the child who wanted to constantly talk about it, I soon realised it wasn't really something you were meant to discuss over a lunch; it was just a part of life that humans tried to ignore. But I like talking about it. I bring it up at parties and people slowly move away from me, while I awkwardly finger the sausage rolls. I got drunk at a friend's wedding recently and whispered to my friend: 'Isn't it bizarre that we don't know what age we'll pop our clogs?' She told me to go and get another red wine and dance to Earth, Wind and Fire.

I wouldn't say I'm obsessed with it, but I think about it a lot. Not in a morbid way either; I have just always been acutely aware of mortality: my own and that of my loved ones. I just like to keep it at the back of my mind. It makes me braver, and less anxious. I realised it might be connected to why I'm alway late (stay with me here): late people, according to a scientific report, strongly believe that 'time is relative and they learn to live in the moment'. It makes sense. My obsession with death is the reason I'm always late, because who cares if we're ten minutes late? We are all going to die eventually so there's no need to get our knickers in a twist.

The Internet has also been a way of reading about grief and processing my own feelings about death. Something that really shook me to the core and made me sit down and think about death properly was a status update posted by Sheryl Sandberg, Facebook's COO, who took to the platform to share her innermost feelings about the tragic death of her husband, Dave. It was the most poignant thing I'd ever read about death. I sat on the sofa in my flat and cried for hours. Not just little sobs but deep painful cries. Through the computer screen I was feeling something extremely powerful, for her, with her. I'd never felt for another person who I'd never met so strongly before. I must have been, in a very small and insignificant way, grieving *for* her.

The Internet and platforms like Facebook have enabled us to share our hardest struggles and make an impact on others. Sheryl included a how-to list of what I can only describe to be *how the fuck to get through it*: 'I appreciate every smile, every hug. I no longer take each day for granted. When a friend told me that he hates birthdays and so he was not celebrating his, I looked at him and said through tears, "Celebrate your birthday, goddammit. You are lucky to have each one."'

I was always someone who hated birthdays. I hate the stress that comes with organising a party, and the fear of how many people will let you down. I read this and took stock of my own life. From someone else's Facebook post. From someone else's experience. From someone I'd never met, thousands of miles away. Because isn't this the point of sharing? Being able to affect someone else's life, for good? Daring to be vulnerable is brave. Daring to speak up about the unspeakable is a powerful thing. We are constantly influenced and affected by people we will never meet.

Thinking about death a lot has not turned me into someone who gets down in the dumps about time ticking. Instead, it has turned me into a productivity machine. I'd be so worried about time going past so quickly that I wouldn't be afraid to just try things. All those moments when your brain tries to persuade you not to attempt something, because it says *who do you think you are?* – I would just do it anyway, because hey, why not? The 'life is too short' voice in my head made me just do things without really thinking them through. They say that a youthful naivety can be the key to getting a foot in the door and I believe that to be true. I was also recently reminded of the lyrics to Gwen Stefani's solo track 'What You Waiting for?' in which she talks about time running out. The whole music video is essentially about being too scared. Because life is scary. 'YOU NEVER KNOW, IT COULD BE GREAT!' was my catchphrase for the next chapter of my life. Thanks Gwen. *Tick tock, tick tock, tick tock.*

I logged into Twitter recently and read the horrible news that a fashion blogger had died. Her Twitter account was linked to an automatic update app, which would robotically post how many new followers she would get each week. Her dad had gone onto her feed to confirm the tragedy and to say that he was accepting messages. But each week the automatic alerts would continue to post to her feed. The Twitterbot would send out an automated post: 'Your followers rising! Seventy-eight new followers this week.' Her dad tweeted to her followers asking if anyone knew how to turn off these alerts because it was horrible to see that her social media feeds were still alive when she wasn't. A similar story came up when I went for lunch with a fellow journalist friend, who told me a friend of hers sadly committed suicide a few years ago. 'It's weird, because on Facebook he still comes up as "liking" different pages.

It's as though his Facebook page was still being used until they realised it must have been an error, and shut it down. It was horrible for the family to see his Facebook page still "doing things".'

Twitter has changed the way we can access the news of a death. When a celebrity name is trending it's normally one of two things: they have died, or they have been announced as a *Strictly Come Dancing* (or insert other reality TV show) contestant. News outlets are also becoming increasingly insensitive about celebrity deaths on Twitter. It's all one big rat race to get the most clicks, the most amount of retweets and the most traffic to their news website. The ethics of the Internet 'clickbait' is questioned, when newspapers do anything to beat their competitors with a cheap article about a famous death and a gratuitous headline.

My first experience with someone I loved dying happened when I was eleven. My nan died and it all happened very quickly. My sister and I were staying over at my grandparents' house one night. Late that evening after we'd gone to bed, my sister and I were sharing headphones while listening to our Discman in their spare room. My nan heard us giggling and came in to tell us to go to sleep; I could tell she wouldn't be able to sleep herself unless we had calmed down. She told us off for trying to 'strangle ourselves' with the headphone wires and took the Discman away from us. Being the worrier she was, everything was dramatised in case we hurt ourselves. She never told us off properly, just in a way that showed how much she cared about us. She would scout out any potential hazards and immediately abolish any chance of anything dangerous happening. Of course, we always did what she said – we loved her more than anything in the world. She was the kindest, gentlest woman I ever knew.

The next morning we heard the news that Nan had been taken into hospital overnight. It had been a stroke, and when we went in to visit her, she looked sad and different and struggled to move half of her face, making it difficult to understand her speech. Because she lived right next door to us, we saw her every single day. Memories started flooding back as I sat with her: all the times she'd taken me to the park, when she'd allow me to take all of her tin cans out of her cupboards and build a shop and sell them all back to her, when she'd let me dress up in all her fancy clothes and hats and vintage sunglasses. She'd often let me pick out a toy from a magazine and she'd knit it for me while I watched the TV. Each toy smelt of her perfume. I also remember calling her in from her bedroom as my usual TV show got interrupted because of the breaking news involving the Twin Towers in 2001. She ran in, and we both sat on the sofa, my hand on her arm, crying our eyes out, together. I'd never seen her cry so much.

Although my nan's death was horrible and I missed her deeply, it is at least a normal thing for your grandparents to be the first in your family or immediate close circle to die. A few years after my nan died, my granddad passed away. I missed his stories about the war, even though I'd heard each one multiple times, I missed watching Fred Astaire and Betty Grable movies with them both, and I missed their dusty ornaments and Battenberg cake. I mourned for their personalities, unique quirks, the bad jokes, our shared memories, the love. But I wasn't angry when they died; I didn't feel like they were robbed of a short life or stolen from me, even though of course I would have loved nothing more than to have had more years with them. But when they started to be in pain, I realised it's often sadder to watch people suffer. The first thing we did on both occasions when they died was go through boxes and boxes of old photos. It was a time to grieve, together, as a family, and chuckle over old embarrassing Polaroids or try to work who was in the background of a photo: 'Is that Auntie Bessie in that strange hat?' 'Dad, is that you as a baby?' There was something incredibly soothing about digging through hard copies of photos, and being able to look back on their lives through a series of things, in front of us, holding the memories in our hands. The photos might have been few and far between, but my goodness they were precious.

On the opposite side of the spectrum, it's rare for someone of our generation to die. One of my sister Jo's close friends, Stevi, passed away suddenly in her second year of university, shaking up Jo's entire world, as well as many, many others close to her. No one is supposed to die at nineteen. No one is supposed to die at university. It's not how life is supposed to happen. I asked Jo about it again recently. Do we mourn differently in the digital age? Does the Internet soothe us, in the face of tragedy?

Although Stevi's close friends were told separately, Stevi's funeral arrangements were also announced on Facebook to her wider friendship network, by her parents. Facebook has become a meeting point for her friends and family. A way to savour all the memories, to receive photos, videos, old school photos, funny self-ies, letters or poems. Maybe a digital grave. The Facebook page, although deeply sad, is full of life, full of colour, full of Stevi's personality. I only met Stevi once, but I find myself on her page frequently now. We are still able to feel close to exactly how she spoke, acted, laughed – and just how many people's lives she affected.

Friends and relatives still write to her and Jo says the act of clicking 'send' is therapeutic for people who miss her. They are still talking to her. Her parents were also able to organise memorial events through Facebook, with all the specifics such as 'please wear some yellow, her favourite colour, to the funeral'. It is a way of keeping in touch with people who want to remember her every day. It is also a way of keeping in touch with her. Four years later, the messages are still being sent and Stevi's memory is very much alive. The Internet really does have its upsides.

It does make me feel as though the Internet can keep us immortalised in ways that were impossible before. It's the photos and videos of people we love that keep us going. Maybe that is a reason in itself to share your life online. There is something wonderful about the idea that you are leaving little pieces of yourself for your loved ones to find in years to come, or for a random stranger to enjoy your writing or pictures a hundred years later.

We all just want to be remembered, don't we?

Fears that go through your mind when writing a book in the social media age:

1. A sentence that you later regret ends up being hand-stitched onto a cushion, sold on Etsy or worse, shared by Pinterest influencers or parenting blogs.

2. A *VICE* staff writer pens a scathing review which results in turning you into nothing but a Tumblr meme for centuries on end.

3. There is a hashtag made of the title of your book trending world wide, but it's not about your book.

4. You notice the cool girl in a beanie hat next to you on the train is Snapchatting their friend the thumbs down emoji and a picture of her holding your book.

5. You see someone reading your book, and then five minutes later opting out to heartlessly play Candy Crush instead.

6. Someone writes a review on their blog which starts off: 'I've not actually read it yet, but …'

7. Emma Watson tweets something about *Ctrl Alt Delete* but then you realise she's actually just trying to reboot her very old computer.

Acknowledgements

To my agent and literary godmother Robyn Drury and everyone at Diane Banks Associates, without whom none of this would be possible. Robyn, I have loved every minute of this journey and so happy to call you a friend. I look forward to working on many more projects with you.

To everyone at Ebury for your unwavering support. First of all, Sara Cywinski: thank you for working your magic, being so good at what you do and believing in the book from day one. Thank you to Tess Henderson, Clarissa Pabi and Grace Paul for being so enthusiastic about the book. Thank you to my friend and talented photographer Holly McGlynn for taking the book's cover photo – it was a fun day.

Gina, David, Sarah and Jo: you are the coolest siblings in the world, I love you all. Jo, thank you for being my very first proofreader of the book. I am so lucky to have you as my partner-in-crime.

To my oldest friends whose honest opinion I can always trust: Emma Whenham and Sophie Whenham (for encouraging me when I first had the idea); Polly Crane (who helped come up with the book title!), Charlotte Clarke (who let me read whole chapters to her while drunk), Georgie Humphries (for your ongoing support) and Grace Dixon (for being a weird teenager with me).

Thank you to Uncle Dave and Tufty for letting me live with you – without you it would have been difficult to take that first internship.

Meera Patel and Amy Croxford, thank you for celebrating with me. Vicki Johnson, Dannii Horgan, Nadia Vere – I love you guys. You'll enjoy page 150.

To the creative women in my life: Katie Oldham, Laura Jane Williams, Megan Gilbride, Alex Cameron and Stevie Martin, it's a privilege to have such strong women around me. Your talents amaze me.

To the inspirational women who gave me pep-talks along the way: Zoe Sugg (for being a #TeamInternet inspiration); Lena Dunham (I will treasure your emails forever); Liz Gilbert (for unknowingly giving me a permission slip) and Ashley C. Ford (for supporting and sharing my writing). Brené Brown for introducing me to the power of vulnerability through your books and talks.

To my friends at TheDebrief.co.uk, thanks for being the funniest and cleverest group of girls I've had the pleasure of working with.

To anyone who has ever read my blog or newsletter, listened to my podcast, tweeted me a nice thing, attended an #IRLPanel event or just generally engaged with my work, thank you. The online writing/blogging community has made me feel like all of this is possible – you know who you are.

To my amazing parents, Will and Sue, who have done so much for me and have always supported my strange and often unconventional choices.

And last but not at all least, my boyfriend Paul for keeping me sane.

I'm so lucky to have you all in my life.